Polycentric mission leadership
organization that wants to wo
Church. This book highlights and unpacks the scholarly thinking
in this field. It is a great read for all who want to get up to speed on this topic. I
believe this way of leading equips us far better if our genuine hope is to help and
not hinder God's missional purposes in the world.

Mary T. Lederleitner, PhD, Executive Director of Missional Intelligence LLC,
author of Cross-Cultural Partnerships *and* Women in God's Mission

I'm happy to endorse both this work and this person. Joe is someone who has a
heart for all of God's people and who is deeply committed to the training up and
empowering of leaders from around the world. For the Lausanne Movement as
well this book is a great snapshot in our ongoing nurturing and supporting and
platforming of global polycentric leadership, community, and collaboration, all
core to the vision for Lausanne 4.

Michael Y. Oh, Ph.D.,
Lausanne Movement Global Executive Director / CEO

Plurality of leadership is clearly God's design both in Old Testament Israel
(elders, judges, priests and prophets as well as kings), and the New Testament
Church. And the history of Christian mission from the earliest centuries has been
shown to be polycentric and multi-directional. Joe Handley's research and
recommendations are timely, indeed one might say long overdue as the day of
uni-directional, Western-centred, hierarchically structured mission enterprise is
long past (not that it was ever really the true or whole picture). His broad analysis
from several sources identifies a range of qualities that polycentric leadership
requires and, when functioning well, actually exhibits. It is encouraging to see
these leadership qualities exemplified (even if imperfectly) in the Lausanne
Movement among others, and important also to add that all of them have
profoundly biblical roots and precedents.

Chris Wright, Langham Partnership

Years ago, the leaders of the World Evangelical Alliance encouraged us to grow
as 'reflective practitioners.' These words accurately describe what Joe Handley
has presented to us in *Polycentric Mission Leadership*. Joe's work is reflective –
integrating well-documented research and theoretical approaches regarding
leading a multi-cultural team. And his work is the voice of a long-term
practitioner – offering practical and implementable ideas of creating an
organizational context where diverse people are empowered and encouraged to
bring their strengths and insights to the table for the benefit of all. *Polycentric
Missions Leadership* is for mission executives, field leaders, and anyone who
cares about leading a culturally diverse team for Kingdom of God impact.

Paul Borthwick, Senior Consultant, Development Associates International,
author of Western Christians in Global Leadership:
What's the Role of the North American Church?

Jesus continues to build his global church! But growth brings challenges. Mission leaders throughout the world regularly discuss leadership tensions affecting the fulfillment of the Great Commission. Eavesdrop on these conversations and you will hear discussions related to ethnicity, diversity, effective communication, conflict, leadership style, cultures, and Western-Majority World partnerships. Few resources, and even fewer highly competent leaders, exist to assist the church with these matters. *Polycentric Mission Leadership* is a fresh paradigm that challenges the status quo! Joe Handley draws deeply from theological, missiological, academic, and personal experience and provides this much needed book. He is my go-to person when it comes to leading global teams! Now this book has been published, eavesdrop on future leadership conversations and you will hear much discussion of polycentric leadership as a necessary way forward!

J. D. Payne, missiologist, author, professor of Christian Ministry, Samford University, Birmingham, Alabama.

If you have spent any amount of time serving the Church in Africa and different parts of the world, then you know that leadership structure plays a significant role in determining what gets accepted and how novel ideas are received and processed. This book articulates a leadership approach which I believe has the potential to empower the Church to be all that it is called to be in these constantly changing times. Joe does a very outstanding job of not only defining but showing us what polycentric leadership could look like in ministry settings. Like the parable of the wine and wineskins, I believe that we should all be constantly giving thought to the nature of the wineskins needed to contain the fresh move of the Spirit as He continues the work of preparing His Bride for His return. Joe's dissertation adds substance to that conversation. I strongly recommend it to Church and ministry leaders.

Delphine Fanfon, Doctor of Strategic Leadership, Africa Leader, LeaderSource

The Significant and rapid changes of the Kingdom landscape demand a new structure, governance, leadership model and style to do and manage mission works internationally in the 21st century. This Kingdom landscape change does not only demand the needs for the rethinking of global mission strategy but also leadership ... [Handley] opens up for a new or newly introduced discourse on structure, governance, management and leadership of international mission organizations for the 21st century.

Bambang Budijanto, Ph.D., Asia Evangelical Alliance General Secretary/CEO

While every observer of world missions currently acknowledges its radically changing context and conditions, too little attention has been given to the nature and shape of leadership in this new complex environment. To this dire need speaks Joe Handley's innovative study which suggests a new paradigm called *Polycentric Mission Leadership*. Drawing from both his vast international and global ministry experience and resources as diverse as secular and Christian leadership theory, Trinitarian theology, and focused interviews of leaders of a prominent global mission agency, among others, Joe presents a compelling and inspiring fresh vision. Highly recommended for all practitioners and academicians interested in the future of Christian ministry in the third millennium.

Veli-Matti Kärkkäinen, Professor of Systematic Theology, Fuller Theological Seminary and Docent of Ecumenics, University of Helsinki, Finland

Leadership is the art of influencing others toward achieving mutually beneficial outcomes, but for missions today that can be seen as something like trying to conduct jazz. For 200 years, traditional missions have been playing from the same score; playing different parts to the same Eurocentric Evangelical melody and rhythm. Now, the decolonising of theology and globalisation of missions is radically changing the beat. New instruments have been joining the stage and the melody is morphing. Recognising this shift, Joe Handley draws on his mission leadership experience and research to propose a way forward for leaders of traditional missions in a new era. Continuing the jazz metaphor, it is an era of multiple instruments with unique tunes, each one authoritative in its own context. As they mix on the global stage, Joe argues that a new breed of leaders is needed – influencers gifted to produce harmony from cacophony. They are participants on stage. Their playing is innovative and visionary. They connect and create space. Their influence is light. Their discernment is keen. Their sole concern is to follow the Holy Spirit in Christ's 'unforced rhythms of grace' to fulfil the mission of God. They are exemplars of polycentric mission leadership.

Dr. Jay Matenga, Director, Global Witness Dept., Executive Director, Mission Commission, World Evangelical Alliance

This book on *Polycentric Mission Leadership* meets a pressing need in this global century of missions from everywhere to everywhere. It provides a roadmap to empower emerging mission structures and to transform existing ones to be cutting edge, nimble, authentic, and innovative. It identifies the kind of value-based global leaders that can spearhead the completion of the Great Commission."

Dr. Mary Ho, International Executive Leader, All Nations International, Inc. |

Joe Handley is a discerning strategist and a skilled practitioner of leadership in a polycentric context. He appreciates the complexities of cross-cultural interactions, and sees the adjustments that global leaders will need to make in their perspectives and in their structures for the world that is coming, and is already here. His observations and insights deserve careful attention.

Rev. David W. Bennett, D.Min.., Ph.D., Global Associate Director for Collaboration & Content The Lausanne Movement

Joe Handley provides an important contribution to our knowledge of the leadership associated with polycentric mission in the 21st century. His study of the Lausanne Movement as a case study of leadership transition documents the emergence of diverse leaders around the world. Building on the ground-breaking work of Allen Yeh, Handley focuses the trained eyes of a leader on the new model he terms polycentric leadership. This is an important work for the global leadership conversation and worthy of broad circulation once published.

Douglas McConnell, Ph.D., Provost Emeritus and Professor of Leadership and Intercultural Studies Fuller Theological Seminary

Joe Handley does a commendable job in taking the principles from my IVP Academic book (2016), *Polycentric Missiology*, and robustly expanding on the principles therein, taking it from the theoretical to concrete application. He has his finger on the future of Christian missional leadership.

Allen Yeh, Ph.D., Associate Professor of Intercultural Studies Department of Intercultural Studies, Biola University

For decades, particularly in the West, Christian organizations have been enamored with the models and methods of successful marketplace corporations. They copied their tenacious pursuit of efficiency and impact all in the effort to serve Christ and his kingdom. But in the process, they also followed the more toxic elements of the marketplace. A cascade of scandals, organizational implosions, and leadership failures is making a new generation of Christians rethink these institutional assumptions. Handley's exploration of polycentric leadership offers a helpful corrective to the toxicity of more top-down, autocratic models while also providing a practical framework for Christian organizations in the interconnected, globalized twenty-first century. Where older models sacrificed health for efficiency, Handley wisely offers a more Christ-like vision of leadership that is both effective and humanizing.

Skye Jethani, author and co-founder of Holy Post Media

Looking for some new ideas on leadership in the complex and changing world of mission? Learn from a veteran. After years of disciplined study and practice, including his own extensive research, Joe Handley has synthesized six primary themes/features of polycentric models of leadership setting forth a vision for leaders in the global community. Learn from a veteran who has been there and done that.

Duane H. Elmer, PhD
Trinity International University/Evangelical Divinity School
G. W. Aldeen Professor of International Studies (Emeritus)
Distinguished Professor of Educational Studies (Retired)

Joe Handley draws you in immediately and keeps you reading at a fast clip, leaving you with plenty to reflect on and apply. Not only does his research draw from a polycentric model of collaborative, communal, diverse, and relational inquiry, his work engages multidisciplinary literature in the fields from Mission, World Christianity, and leadership studies. This short book is comprehensive without being dense – thorough in exploring the literature from different regions of the world and managing to name many of the leading lights in mission and world Christianity studies. His survey also interfaces with contemporary disruptive events that make the need for a polycentric model of missional leadership even more vital. As a professor of mission studies and world Christianity, this will be an important little text to orient my graduate students as they seek relevant models of leadership in mission work.

Wanjiru M Gitau, Assistant Professor of Practical Theology and World Christianity, Palm Beach Atlantic University, and author of
Megachurch Christianity Reconsidered: Millennials and Social Change in African Perspective *(IVP, 2018)*

Polycentric Mission Leadership

Series Preface

Regnum Studies in Mission are born from the lived experience of Christians and Christian communities in mission, especially but not solely in the fast growing churches among the people of the developing world. These churches have more to tell than stories of growth. They are making significant impacts on their cultures in the cause of Christ They are producing 'cultural products' which express the reality of Christian faith, hope and love in their societies.

Regnum Studies in Mission are the fruit often of rigorous research to the highest international standards and always of authentic Christian engagement in the transformation of people and societies. These are for the world. The formation of Christian theology, missiology and practice in the twenty-first century will depend to a great extent on the active participation of growing churches contributing biblical and culturally appropriate expressions of Christian practice to inform World Christianity.

Regnum is supported by the generosity of EMW

Polycentric Mission Leadership

Toward a New Theoretical Model
for Global Leadership

Joseph W. Handley, Jr.

British Library Cataloguing in Publication Data
A catalogue record for this book is available from the British Library

ISBN: 978-1-5064-9742-6
eBook ISBN: 978-1-5064-9743-3

Cover image based on the Polycentric Leadership website logo:
https://polycentricleadership.com

. Typeset by Words by Design

Distributed by 1517 Media in the US, Canada, India, and Brazil

Dedication

This thesis is dedicated to my parents, Joe and Pat Handley, who laid the foundation for my life, ministry and leadership. They are the inspiration behind the way I lead, modelling the essence of what unfolds in the following chapters. The impact they have on me, my family, ministry and life is profound. I am forever grateful for this rich legacy the Lord provided to me through them.

Contents

Preface: A World in Tension

The past 18 months have been one of the most disruptive seasons of my life. We have all been deeply impacted by a global pandemic, one of the worst economic downturns of the century, and a divisive political environment (whether in the US, ongoing troubles in Afghanistan, or the Ukraine crisis). We faced lockdowns, a loss of incomes and jobs, and the COVID-19 pandemic.

I began 2020 with high hopes and aspirations, only to find that I would be stuck in one location for longer than I had at any time for the last 30 years. I didn't catch a bus or a train, or drive anywhere from my neighborhood in Tokyo for months on end other than to the local market. I lived on digital technology and watched what appeared to be a planet spiraling into oblivion.

When I moved back to Los Angeles in December 2020, it felt like I had entered a different planet than the one I left five years prior. My home state, California, had stricter quarantine restrictions than Tokyo, and yet many people didn't abide by the regulations. In Japan, most people followed the guidelines, but the US individualist society sees things quite differently. There is something called a "cowboy" nature that sometimes comes out in those of us who live in the US. We question authority and want autonomy above all else. I found my new setting chaotic, difficult to thrive in, and even more challenging to lead in.[1]

My Leadership Journey and Influences

My mission journey began with watching my parents provide leadership in our home, church, business, and on short-term mission trips. This family-style leadership provides the backdrop for how I flesh out Polycentric Mission Leadership in the pages that follow.

As I reflect on my life, I am struck with how many people and events have shaped who I am as a mission leader today. One of those people was my father. Coming to faith in high school, he left his Montana home to attend Life Bible College in California. After graduating, he served as a lay pastor for several years before going into business for himself as a roofing contractor. He often

---

[1] This section is an adaptation of an article presented for *Outcomes Magazine*. Handley, Joseph. "Polycentric Leadership: A Leadership Model for a Polarized World," *Outcomes Magazine*: Christian Leadership Alliance, Spring 2021 – https://outcomesmagazine.com/polycentric-leadership/ (accessed on 6 March 2021).

spoke about how he had more opportunities to lead others to Christ as a business owner than he had as a pastor.

As a young boy, I would spend a lot of time with my father during school breaks, joining him as he did roofing estimates, collected payments, and interacted with customers. As I watched my dad, I observed certain values like integrity, hard work, and compassion. As I got older he would occasionally leave me with a work crew on the roof so I could learn the nuts and bolts of the business. I learned more than just how to tar and shingle a roof, though. Those years of working with my father and his crew shaped my view of leadership and service as I learned how to work on a team, give and take, and serve together to accomplish a task.

My sister Suzy also shaped my view of mission leadership. Her autism profoundly affected our family as I was growing up and I would often watch on as my mother served as her devoted advocate, always looking out for what was best for her. This sometimes meant changing churches to be in a place that offered services for Suzy. At the time, I thought it was unfair that I couldn't stay at the same church as my friends. In one such experience, we went from a Pentecostal Foursquare Gospel church to a Quaker Meeting. Going from a "full Gospel" experience, as some would call it, to the quiet, more meditative Quaker fellowship was quite an adjustment! Little did I know, however, how God would use those experiences to shape me into a more compassionate person.

To add more diversity to my denominational experiences, I attended a conservative Baptist middle and high school. Upon graduating, I attended Azusa Pacific University (APU), which comes from a Wesleyan/Holiness tradition theologically. While there, I continued to go to church with my parents and sister, who were now attending an Evangelical Free Church. Later, I followed my then girlfriend (who later became my wife) to a Wesleyan Church.

My colleagues at APU would provide the collaborative ecosystem that firmly shaped my leadership approach. They embodied a team leadership style that continues with me to this day. It was while I was at APU that my passion for mission was ignited. A friend invited me to join him on a mission trip to Mexico, which changed how I saw myself and the world. Whereas I had initially pursued business and psychology with aspirations of becoming wealthy, I now had a new focus – God's mission. After working in a psychiatric hospital for a few years post-graduation, APU hired me to lead a mission congress similar to the Urbana Student Leadership Conference, but for high school students. It was there that I saw God's hand in so many diverse ways and in so many different denominations.

When I attended the first task force for the congress, I was surprised to discover that the men and women came from nearly every denominational background I had experienced. Their leadership styles reflected their church traditions and I realized God had given me a rich experience of different denominational backgrounds for such a time as this. What I had previously thought unfair was what God used to shape me for a life of mission leadership I would have never anticipated or dreamt about.

At APU, I was also placed in a key role from an early age and began networking with mission leaders around the world. Through their influence, those leaders lifted my eyes to the world of mission that I was only vaguely aware of at the time. The only mission biography I had read up to this point was a classic my mother had given me in middle school: *Hudson Taylor's Spiritual Secret*.

Later, I joined my colleagues and accompanying missionary family from Rolling Hills Covenant Church (RHCC) in delving into the riches of pastoral and mission leadership. While at RHCC, I grew deeply in my understanding of pastoral and mission leadership and went through a profound transformation in my missional focus: from mobilization to empowerment and partnership. It was 1998 and the world was rapidly changing. I soon realized that the church was growing faster outside the West than within it – a revelation that would lead me to Asian Access, where I have since had the most life-changing shifts in my paradigms of mission leadership.

My colleagues at Asian Access have shaped my proposed Polycentric Mission Leadership model and approach like no other. I am blessed beyond measure by the powerful cloud of witnesses with whom I have the privilege of serving alongside – and who have allowed me to understand more fully what it means to be a Polycentric Mission Leader (a term I will flesh out in later chapters).

It is important to note that this has been a collaborative journey. First, a few family members and colleagues have journeyed with me in reviewing the research. These have included my wife Silk, my son John, and my colleagues Noel Becchetti, John Houlette, and Mike Wilson.

My doctoral committee and outside readers also played an important role in challenging my assumptions, encouraging further research, and exploring new avenues to deepen my proposed concept. My mentor Doug McConnell led the way, giving special attention to analysing leadership theory. David Bennett suggested the Lausanne Movement as the ideal ecosystem to test the new theory using qualitative interviews, and Allen Yeh catalyzed what I would call the breakthrough idea. His work on Polycentric Missiology took the research to an entirely new level. Spending time with Allen and interacting with him brought a theoretical idea to light – namely, that *a world in need of polycentric approaches necessitates a new form of leadership*.

Bambang Budijanto and Francis Tsui served as outside readers, giving texture and depth to the research, especially reviewing the model from a non-Western perspective. Having their eyes refine the research was particularly insightful given that the study was looking at operating in a global context.

I am grateful for all of these leaders, friends, and family members.

1. Toward a New Theoretical Leadership Model

Introduction

We live in a time of unrivaled global complexity. Political upheavals are occurring in several countries, and ongoing warfare continues unabated. Pressures created by chronic unemployment, income inequality, and refugee migration are on the rise. South Asia and the Middle East face rising religious tensions, bringing societal polarities into sharp relief. Russia and China are seeking to extend their reach, bolster their influence, and pressure their neighbors into submission. On top of these, the rapid challenges we face for climate change and the impact on the environment are troubling.

And the speed of change magnifies these complexities. New technologies designed to connect us also divide us. Social and behavioral norms are in rapid transition where different value systems challenge tradition. For the Global Church, this era of complexity requires that we discern new ways to engage the world around us and discover fresh ways of approaching leadership.

Sherwood Lingenfelter, an anthropologist and former provost at Fuller Seminary, identified a core ingredient to leadership in this new century: "The complexity of leading cross-culturally lies in the challenge of building a community of trust among people who come from two or more cultural traditions."[1] Lamin Sanneh, renowned Yale University professor of World Christianity, affirmed this reality, stating, "Christianity has become ambicultural as the faith of multiple language users straddling national and social boundaries."[2] The world is experiencing more cross-national and intercultural interaction in the fields of commerce, government, education, and faith traditions than at any point in history. The issues of racism and post-colonialism only exacerbate the relational challenges leaders continue to face. Given the new interdependence (along with a growing sense of national identity and tribalism), intercultural competence is critical and, as Lingenfelter advocated, fostering communities of trust is foundational to leading well interculturally.

Lingenfelter also highlighted the need for teamwork, which was illustrated by Ronald Heifetz and Marty Linsky in *Leadership on the Line,* where they underscored "working in teams" as an important dimension of leadership for

---

[1] Lingenfelter, Sherwood. *Leading Cross-Culturally: Covenant Relationships for Effective Christian Leadership.* Grand Rapids, MI: Baker, 2008, 20.
[2] Sanneh, Lamin. *The Changing Face of Christianity: Africa, the West, and the World.* Oxford: Oxford University Press, 2005, 214.

the future. Heifetz and Linsky believe that, "Hierarchical structures with clearly defined roles are giving way to more horizontal organizations with greater flexibility, room for initiative and corresponding uncertainty. Democratization is spreading throughout organizations as well as countries."[3] This theme is captured by many current postmodern and emerging church models[4] and is also present in the way emerging generations lead.[5] Given the chaotic, rapidly changing pace of the modern world, flexible, contextually appropriate models of leadership are essential.

Reggie McNeal also captured these challenges for mission leaders: "We do not live in normal times. You may have noticed that we are in a vortex of transitional forces that are creating a new world. We need great leaders to help us get through the wormhole of overlapping universes."[6] James Kouzes and Barry Posner added: "We have said that leaders take us to places we have never been before. But there are no freeways to the future, no paved highways to unknown, unexplored destinations. There is only wilderness. If you are to step into the unknown, the place to begin is with the exploration of the inner territory."[7] The environment that McNeal, Kouzes, and Posner described necessitates a new look at how to lead given the complexities before us. They highlight the importance of self-awareness and inner work as well as a grasp of context and culture.

My goal is to find a better approach to leadership in a world where everything – from supply chains to political conflict to the church – is global. Drawing from my personal experience in mission leadership, the works of my colleagues from Azusa Pacific University, Rolling Hills Covenant, and Asian Access, and a wealth of academic research in fields as diverse as mission history and research on governance, I am proposing what I hope is a useful new model for leadership. Instead of the centralized or "statist" approach

---

[3] Heifetz, Ronald and Marty Linsky. *Leadership on the Line: Staying Alive through the Dangers of Leading*. Cambridge, MA: Harvard, 2002, 4. There is some data showing that democratic governance has flatlined in countries since 2000. See Max Roser (2020) – "Democracy". Published online. Retrieved 12, March 2020. and Marshall, Monty and Gabrielle Elzinga Marshall, Global Report 2017: Conflict, Governance and State Fragility. Center for Systemic Peace, 2017. Given the challenges highlighted in this chapter, this flatlining could prove to be a disturbing trend, one that highlights the importance of the thesis of this dissertation.

[4] McManus, Erwin. *An Unstoppable Force: Daring to become the Church God had in Mind*. Colorado Springs, CO: David C. Cook, 2001.

[5] Bennis, Warren and Robert Thomas. *Geeks and Geezers: How Era, Values and Defining Moments Shape Leaders*. Boston, MA: Harvard Business School Press, 2002.

[6] McNeal, Reggie. *Practicing greatness: 7 Disciplines of Extraordinary Spiritual Leaders*. San Francisco, CA: Jossey-Bass, 2006, 5.

[7] Kouzes, James M., and Barry Z. Posner. *The Leadership Challenge: How to Keep Getting Extraordinary Things Done in Organizations*. San Francisco, CA: Jossey-Bass, 1995, 302.

people often associate with corporate CEOs, I envision a model of leadership that is *polycentric* – leadership that is collaborative, taking input from a rich diversity of sources in order to achieve better and more representative outcomes than the traditional top-down hierarchical or managerial approach to leadership that has been prevalent for decades. Over and above collaboration, decentralized leadership allows for each region of the world and every sector of a company to make decisions that are just in time and appropriate for the local context. In this way, agency is empowered through different centers, allowing better choices to be made that are relevant to the local situation.

In developing this new model of what I call Polycentric Mission Leadership, the Lausanne Movement and the 2010 congresses celebrating the centennial of the famed Edinburgh Missionary Conference in 1910 provided a background and ecosystem for my research. I focused interviews for the research behind this theory (shared in Chapter Five) primarily on the Lausanne Movement because it provided a rich ecosystem for studying leadership in global mission. The Lausanne Movement is a remarkable story that is filled with ebbs and flows, yet one that has helped to form the contours of world mission during the current era. Lausanne has been shaped by a wide variety of leaders from different backgrounds and styles, providing a unique laboratory within which to review theoretical models for leadership in mission. Beyond the influence of leaders, the movement draws from an array of networks and organizations committed to the same cause, which adds to the complexity of the leadership dynamic, providing further dimensions to review for theoretical testing.

My assessment of the influence of the polycentric model was done primarily in the context of the Lausanne Movement. The movement began when charismatic leader Billy Graham partnered with John Stott, a reflective practitioner, and Jack Dain, a strategic coordinator. The movement ebbed and flowed with the coming and going of various leaders and came to a period of near silence after the Second International Congress in Manila in 1989. The movement was rekindled at a meeting in Pattaya in 2004, where Paul Cedar, chair of the Lausanne Movement at the time, suggested that a man named Doug Birdsall take over leadership of the movement. The following years led to a resurgence of the movement with momentum building up to the Third International Congress in Cape Town in 2010, where more than 4,000 Christian leaders came together.

Post-Cape Town, many questioned the viability of the movement and its future until a leader named Michael Oh was appointed as CEO and a new era began. Under his leadership, the movement shifted to a more organizational identity. Today, the movement seems to have regained momentum, but this has not been without its challenges, and the questions of longer-term viability and sustainability remain. As the mission world shifts toward a more polycentric order, will a polycentric model of leadership prove more fruitful overall? My study of polycentric leadership that I lay out in the following pages will analyze these dynamics and establish the contours of a polycentric model of leadership emerging in the present era of mission.

In Chapter 2, I provide an overview of the recent work on polycentrism in other fields. The Munich School of World Christianity contributed to a re-thinking of the history of Christian missions along polycentric lines. Its scholars argue that the history of missions is a lot less one-directional (the West to the rest) than commonly thought. Instead, from the missionary work in sub-Saharan Africa to the spread of Christianity in Korea, missions have tended to be from "everywhere to everywhere".

In Chapter 3, I look at models of leadership in a secular context to bolster the case for a polycentric model. The two most important contributions in this area are from economist Elinor Ostrom's work on polycentric governance[8] and the empirical evidence from the GLOBE study of CEO leadership.[9] J.R. Woodward[10] and Wycliffe Global Alliance director Kirk Franklin provide a sort of bridge between these two areas by calling for a new framework for mission leadership.[11] Together with the growing relevance of polycentrism in missiology and compelling evidence for decentralized leadership in the secular world, Woodward and Franklin's work points towards a new theoretical model for mission leadership: polycentric leadership.

In Chapter 4, I reveal the theoretical model Polycentric Mission Leadership. Synthesizing the research on polycentric structures with the evidence from polycentric governance and the GLOBE study (a comprehensive study of leaders around the world identifying key aspects of effective leadership), I identify six key themes that characterize strong polycentric leadership. Leadership must be collaborative, communal, diverse, allow for entrepreneurial freedom, be relational, and be charismatic.

After describing each of the six themes, I move on to the evaluation phase of my research in Chapter 5. This consists of several interviews I conducted with leaders from the Lausanne Movement. Using the content of these interviews, I determined to what extent global mission leadership today in the Lausanne Movement reflects polycentrism.

I conclude in Chapter 6 by reviewing the theoretical concept of Polycentric Mission Leadership and pointing to strengths and weaknesses that require further study. Here, I pull the research together and present the new model in

---

[8] Ostrom, Elinor. "Beyond markets and states: polycentric governance of complex economic systems." *American Economic Review*, 100 (3): June 2010, 641–72.
[9] House, Robert J., Peter W. Dorfman, Mansour Javidian, Paul J. Hanges, and Mary F. Sully de Luque. *Strategic Leadership Across Cultures: The GLOBE Study of CEO Leadership Behavior and Effectiveness in 24 countries*. Thousand Oaks, CA: Sage Publications, 2014.
[10] Woodward, J.R. *Creating a Missional Culture: Equipping the Church for the Sake of the World*. Downers Grove, IL: InterVarsity Press, 2012.
[11] Franklin, Kirk James. *A Paradigm for Global Mission Leadership: The Journey of the Wycliffe Global Alliance*. Oxford: Regnum, 2016.

the context of the literature and research, setting the stage for the exploration of this emergent leadership theory.

Summary of the Research

This research presents a Polycentric Mission Leadership model that brings together findings from Polycentric Missiology, The Munich School of World Christianity, the Bloomington School at Indiana University on polycentric governance, and social movements, analyzing their relevance for the Lausanne Movement from 2000 to the present. To provide context and further substance to the study, these findings were juxtaposed alongside research done among Lausanne Movement leaders. Comparing the findings with the research from the GLOBE study supplements the results by providing quantitative measurements assessing global leadership, which strengthens the new theoretical model. Alongside the Lausanne Movement research, I looked at Peter Northouse's approach to assessing leadership theories in order to determine the viability of the new theoretical model.[12]

Sure enough, a polycentric theory of leadership emerged, which has at its core principles that are relevant, reliable, and worthy of further review within mission leadership studies. The contention of this thesis is that this theoretical framework, first mentioned as a concept by Woodward and later Franklin, presents a polycentric theory that can be explored by future generations of scholars and researchers. Franklin and Nelus Niemandt describe this new idea well:

> Through polycentrism, there is a movement to lessen the potential autocratic effects of established centres of power, in terms of structure and centralisation in the midst of decentralisation, by means of a bottom-up approach with some degree of control. The results are: (1) one leads from among and with others; (2) one leads from creatively learning together in community and to attentiveness to the others in the community; and (3) one leads within the margins of the global church.[13]

The idea formulated here is what I sought to explore. As Franklin and Niemandt state at the outset of the same paper:

> Structures for mission have been under review as a result of many factors. In particular, [there] have been the widening influences of globalisation, and to a lesser degree, glocalisation. Various models of leadership praxis and structures have been proposed along the way. As Christianity moved farther away from the

---

[12] Northouse, Peter. *Leadership: Theory and Practice*. Thousand Oaks, CA: Sage, 2013.
[13] Franklin, Kirk & Niemandt, N. "Polycentrism in the *Missio Dei*," *HTS Teologiese Studies / Theological Studies*. 72, 2, 2016.

Christendom model of centralised control to other models of structure and leadership, other paradigms have been proposed along the way. However, one possibility, called the concept of polycentrism, has not been considered with any significant effort.[14]

In the following pages I develop a foundation for a Polycentric Mission Leadership model. What the findings reveal is a set of common themes that arise from a various schools of thought that offer a new contribution in the field of polycentrism. While these schools approach polycentrism in diverse fashion (national, regional, organizational, ethnic, gender based, etc.), when reviewed as a whole, they provide a strong dataset for a new polycentric theoretical mission leadership model comprised of major themes. Just as Frans Johansson found innovation developing from what he called the *Medici Effect*, I see polycentrism as a model that allows for a diversity of ideas and perspectives to interact with one another.[15] Johansson noted that this effect is what brought significant breakthroughs and innovations to the modern world. In much the same way, polycentric leadership may provide a fresh approach that leads to creative solutions in the world of mission today.

---

[14] Franklin & Neimandt, 2016, 1.

[15] Johansson, Frans. *The Medici Effect: Breakthrough Insights at the Intersection of Ideas, Concepts, and Cultures*. Boston, MA: Harvard Business School, 2004.

2. Polycentric Mission History and Missiology

Introduction

To best understand the dynamics of global mission leadership today, it's important to review the context and history of mission movement and development over the past century and see how leadership theory may apply. With that in mind, I began my research by looking at how the perspectives of mission historians have changed in recent decades.

In order to understand the importance of Polycentric Mission Leadership, it helps to review the way mission developed over time. Early on, I learned that modern mission history was characterized by heroes, especially the likes of William Carey, Hudson Taylor, Cam Townsend, and Donald McGavran.[1] For the novice missionary, it appeared that mission history was catalyzed by these giants of the faith – people who took the initiative and launched an entire enterprise. Carey was the premier champion taking the gospel to the coastlands of India. Taylor, who founded the China Inland Mission (today OMF), pioneered the era of taking the good news to the inlands beyond the coastal regions. Finally, McGavran and Townsend led the era focused on unreached people groups. While these stories were inspirational, during my research I learned of a whole new way of looking at mission history and its polycentric antecedents.

Mission historian Kenneth Scott Latourette labeled 1792–1910 as "the great century of missions".[2] As part of this "great century", many have called William Carey the "father of the modern mission movement". While Count Nikolaus von Zinzendorf preceded Carey, it was Carey's *An Enquiry Into the Obligation of Christians to Use Means for the Conversion of the Heathens* that catalyzed a mission movement.[3] In fact, Carey pioneered the use of demographics to identify the current state of mission growth. In addition, the Great Commission became central in mission as Carey highlighted "make disciples" as the primary verb in Matthew 28. Finally, Carey encouraged the formation of mission societies based on his awareness of Catholic missional

---

[1] Winter, Ralph. "Four Men, Three Eras," *Mission Frontiers*. Sept 1997.

[2] Latourette, Kenneth Scott. *A History of the Expansion of Christianity: The great century, A.D. 1800-A.D. 1914, Europe and the United States of America*. New York: Harper and Brothers, 1938.

[3] Carey, William. *An Enquiry into the Obligation of Christians to use Means for the Conversion of the Heathens*. Whitefish, MT: Kessenger Publications, 2010.

orders.[4] Samuel Moffett offers: "But for enduring global missionary impact, no rapid sequence of events in the history of Protestant missions can match what was accomplished in only 13 months between May 1792 and June 1793. In that one year four incidents of great consequence, all involving William Carey, changed the history of modern missions."[5]

Carey had a special relationship with Andrew Fuller, a theologian who helped strengthen Carey's missional theories. Carey suggested in 1810 that they hold an ecumenical missions conference at the Cape of Good Hope in South Africa.[6] One hundred years later this suggestion came to fruition in Edinburgh, Scotland. Interestingly enough, the organizers of the Third Lausanne International Congress (otherwise known as Cape Town 2010) quietly but intentionally drew upon Carey's original conference idea – in 2010![7]

Prior to looking at the work on Polycentric Missiology, I had not considered the idea of polycentric leadership.[8] However, Allen Yeh presented a plausible case for why mission has become polycentric in nature over the last 100 years. It was his study that prompted deeper reflection about the Lausanne Movement and how it has developed over time. That insight opened the door for a new set of research questions which will be addressed later by analysing polycentric structures. I also discovered a strain of study that flows from the Munich School of World Christianity,[9] which posits that mission history is less unidimensional than is portrayed in historical mission studies. These literature reviews, when considered as a collective, reveal a more polycentric theory for mission leadership.

Mission History

Klaus Koschorke begins the first chapter of a compendium on "Polycentric Structures in the History of World Christianity" by telling a story about Portuguese missionary to India Vasco da Gama:

---

[4] Yeh, Allen. Interview, Biola University, February 4, 2015.

[5] Moffett, Samuel. *The History of Christianity in Asia*. Maryknoll, NY: Orbis, 2005, 254.

[6] Latourette, Kenneth Scott. "Ecumenical Bearings of the Missionary Movement and the International Missionary Council," in Ruth Rouse and Stephen C. Neill, eds., *A History of the Ecumenical Movement*, vol. 1. Geneva: World Council of Churches, 1954, 355, n. 2.

[7] Yeh, 2015. Also see Latourette, 1954, 355.

[8] Yeh, Allen. *Polycentric Missiology: 21st Century Mission from Everyone to Everywhere*. Downers Grove, IL: IVP Academic, 2016.

[9] Koschorke, Klaus and Hermann, Adrian. *Polycentric Structures in the History of World Christianity*. Berlin: Harrassowitz Verlag, 2014.

Upon da Gama's arrival in India in 1498, he was asked, "What the devil are you looking for?" to which he famously replied, "Christians and spices". Da Gama was surprised to learn that there was already an established church in India, the St Thomas Church.[10]

This small misunderstanding underpins the field of polycentric mission history that has been pioneered by the Munich School and led by Koschorke and others. It challenges the preconception that the history of mission is predominantly a history of Western missionaries traveling to the rest of the world to spread Christianity. Instead, this work finds that mission has always been polycentric – to borrow a phrase from Yeh, not "from the West to the rest", but "from everywhere to everywhere." Below I outline some of the major contributions of the Munich School in developing a mission history that accounts for the key role played by non-Western Christians and missionaries in the historical spread of Christianity.

Koschorke's story illustrates that the history of Christianity in India is more complex than the one-sided account of da Gama as a mission hero bringing Christianity from abroad. It developed from various sources rather than just through Carey. For example, the pre-existing St Thomas Church had been in India long before the Portuguese missionaries. In fact, St Thomas Christians have been in India continuously since the third century! This same pattern is present outside of India as well. For instance, when Francis Xavier arrived in Asia in 1542, he also ran into pre-existing Christian communities. Inspired by cases like these, Munich School historians broadened their scope in searching how mission history developed. This led them to develop a concept known as *polycentric structures* to explain how mission advanced over time and formed in various contexts around the world. They review the history of a number of regions, pointing to structures like missionary societies, denominations, international business ventures, and indigenous networks that tell the fuller story of mission history. In other words, rather than focusing on telling the stories of pioneering missionary legends or of one nation leading the charge, they argue that mission has advanced in a multifaceted manner that includes both external and internal movements.

The more you look, the more you find examples of Christianity growing in a polycentric manner. Sierra Leone is a prime example: freed black slaves became missionaries from North America and established "the first Protestant church in tropical Africa" there in 1792.[11] Instead of being a predominantly Western imposition, this shows that the beginning of Christianity in Sierra Leone revolved around "a ready-made African church, with its own power

---

[10] Koschorke, 2014, 15.

[11] Walls, Andrew. "Sierra Leone, Afro-American Reimmigration and the Beginnings of Protestantism in West Africa," quoted in Koschorke, "Transcontinental Links, Enlarged Maps, and Polycentric Structures in the History of World Christianity," *Journal of World Christianity,* 6/1, 2016: 21.

structures and leadership".[12] These findings portray a different reality of how mission history formed. Rather than being unidirectional, it was a circuitous, polycentric formation. Mission historian Jehu Hanciles concurs as he reflects on the history of Christianity in Africa as a whole: "As the African story indicates, the globalization of Christianity was decidedly polycentric."[13] John Thornton reached similar conclusions in his research, noting that the history of mission is not as simple as Western missionaries coming to the continent. Rather, he notes how mission history is more complex than what has been described, sharing how Christians were taken to the Americas from Africa, some of whom returned as missionaries to their original continent in mission.[14] While it is assumed that Christianity was brought to Africa by Western colonizers, in truth many of the first missionaries to Africa were African or had African origins themselves. Africa is a provocative case study that indicates that the growth of the church worldwide has been far less "from the West to the rest" than "from everywhere to everywhere".

Mission history is replete with examples of mission developing from various poles: external cross-cultural influences, internal/external exchanges, migration, and elites crossing paths in multitudes of locations. Heinrich Bedford-Strohm, German theologian from the Munich School, highlighted what may be a tipping point in how mission history is perceived in the future: "The fact that the Roman Catholic Church chose an Argentinian as their new pope is a sign of hope far beyond denominational lines. It could prove to be historical in being the first prominent expression of the movement from a monocentric church to polycentric church."[15] Peter Tze Ming Ng, another Munich School historian, provided examples from China, noting the indigenous explosion of Christianity and the key role that "the Chinese YMCA in Japan" played in "arousing Chinese [international] students' interest in Christianity".[16] Adrian Harmann showed further examples of international linkages, where "transnational networks" foster evangelism:

> Next to the networks of Ethiopianism, the international connections forged through the YMCA and the World Student Christian Federation, as well as the different Missionary Societies in India, Japan, Korea, etc., the contacts between different independent Catholic churches in the Philippines, Ceylon, Goa, etc.

---

[12] Walls, 2016, 21.

[13] Hanciles, Jehu J. *Beyond Christendom: Globalization, African Migration and the Transformation of the West.* Maryknoll, NY: Orbis Books, 2008.

[14] Thornton, JK. *Africa and Africans in the Making of the Atlantic World, 1400–1800.* Cambridge: Cambridge University Press, 1998, 254, 262.

[15] Beford-Strohm, Heinrich. "Global Christianity as the Horizon of Ecclesial Practice," in Koschorke, and Hermann, 2014, 70.

[16] Ng, Peter Tze Ming. "The Making of Modern China: Reflections on the Role of Chinese YMCA Christians who Returned from Japan and the US in the Early 20th Century," in Koschorke and Hermann, 2014, 133.

have to be considered as an important aspect of an emerging indigenous-Christian public sphere in the polycentric history of global Christianity.[17]

The fact that the YMCA came up in examples from both China and the Philippines is indicative of an overall trend: the YMCA is a clear example of polycentrism and polycentric leadership in mission history. Most examples from mission history merely highlight the need for polycentrism because that is how missions in fact unfolded, but the YMCA is an example of a polycentric leadership model in action. Leaders from China, Japan, and Korea played an active role in the development of mission in several countries: Korea, India, and much of East and Southeast Asia. In his work on the subject, Hartmut Lehmann referred to these as "multipolar" networks because they run through a single organization (the YMCA) rather than multiple independent organizations as you might expect from "pure" polycentrism.[18] Nevertheless, this is still a clear example of polycentric leadership. Whether the effort is multipolar, through one organization like the YMCA, or polycentric, involving a variety of movements working in concert, the diversity of leadership within and throughout a movement is key to fostering the global strength of the movement.

Afe Adogame, speaking about reverse mission in Europe, captured the overall tone of this research quite well: "We are increasingly challenged by research exploring complex historical trajectories and sociocultural processes to illuminate the polycentricity of Christianity."[19] He further stated that we have an "appreciation of the multicultural nature of Christianity in the twenty-first century ... Missions changed from unilateral to multilateral."[20]

The Munich School, and the broader field of Polycentric Missiology that Yeh discusses in his book are not without their critics, however. Some have challenged the Munich School scholars to explore their thesis in further depth. This has led the research in a few different directions. For instance, Adrian Hermann and Ciprian Burlacioiu stressed that the research should be done in concert with other historical perspectives in a recent review of mission history.[21] In fact, the *Journal of World Christianity* recently devoted an entire volume to exploring polycentric structures in mission history in further

---

[17] Hermann, Adrian "Transnational Networks of Philippine Intellectuals," in Koschorke and Hermann, 2014, 202.

[18] Lehmann, Hartmut. "Polyzentrische Strukturen in der Geschichte des Weltchristentums als Forschungsprogramm. Ein Kommentar," in Koschorke and Hermann, 2014, 378.

[19] Adogame, Afe. "African 'Retro-Mission' in Europe," in Koschorke and Hermann, 2014, 307.

[20] Adogame, 316.

[21] Hermann, Adrian and Ciprian Burlacioiu, "Current Debates About the Approach of the 'Munich School' and Further Perspectives on the Interdisciplinary Study of the History of World Christianity." *Journal of World Christianity*, 6 (1), 2016, 67.

depth.[22] Furthermore, mission scholars have uncovered more evidence for polycentric development of Christianity in their study of *Theology and Mission for World Christianity*. Mission historian David Maxwell summarized some of their research, stating, "It is no longer possible to write an account of the church in the last century that places Europe and North America at the center of the study."[23]

This multilateral development contrasts with those stories that inspired me years ago: that mission was inspired and led by famous heroes in mission history. Clearly, polycentrism was part of the process of mission advance over the past century and beyond.

Polycentric Missiology

Yeh draws on mission history to develop a theory of *Polycentric Missiology*. The background to his research is pivotal to understanding the rationale behind forming a new theory for leadership. But Yeh also lays the foundation for the interviews conducted in my study of the Lausanne Movement. Yeh begins with the familiar point that, "A century ago, mission was unilateral and unidirectional 'from the West to the rest.' Today, in light of the phenomenon known as World Christianity, mission is polycentric and polydirectional: 'from everyone to everywhere.'"[24] Yeh notes that this same idea was presented in a *festschrift* to honor mission theologian Tite Tiénou. Momentum has been building for some time for a more polycentric missiology.[25]

Yeh's work provides the link between polycentric mission history and missiology by viewing the historic mission congresses through the lens of polycentrism. The book is devoted to five of the significant mission congresses in 2010 and one in 2012 – all of which Yeh attended himself. He highlights the influence of the original Edinburgh Missionary Conference (1910), noting the development of ideas over the subsequent 100 years that led to the conferences of 2010 and 2012.

The original Edinburgh event was more triumphant in nature, with the expectation that the world would be reached within their generation. As Yeh reviewed the events between 1910 and 2010, one of the common themes he identified is that Christianity has become a truly global religion: "Christianity is the only religion in the world that does not have a geographic center or an ethnic majority. World Christianity validates Christianity much more than a

---

[22] *The Journal of World Christianity*, 6 (1), 2016.
[23] Maxwell, David. "Historical Perspectives on Christianity Worldwide: Connections, Comparisons and Consciousness," in *Theology and Mission in World Christianity*, v. 7. Eds. Cabrita, Maxwell, and Wild-Wood. Leiden: Brill, 2017, 47.
[24] Yeh, 2016.
[25] Yeh, Allen. "Tokyo 2010 and Edinburgh 2010: A Comparison of Two Centenary Congresses," *IJFM* 27:3, Fall, 2010, 117.

Western-only Christianity does. If there is a real God, it makes sense he would be a global God."[26] By 2010, nearly 25 different mission conferences were looking back on the legacy of Edinburgh 1910 – the five 2010 Lausanne congresses being the most prominent. Yeh recognizes the overriding themes for each century: "If the nineteenth century was the *Great Century of Missions* and the twentieth century was the *Great Century of Ecumenism*, then perhaps the twenty-first century is the *Great Century of World Christianity*."[27]

Yeh also walks us through the current state of Christianity and the church, arguing that the various expressions of theology and faith within the Christian movement call for a more pluralistic and inclusive approach to missiology. Yeh shares Johansson's perspective from the *Medici Effect*, arguing that just as "the wealthy Medici family in Florence ... brought together a cross-section of sculptors, scientists, posts, philosophers, financiers, painters, and architects ... [who] found each other, learned from one another and broke down barriers between disciplines and cultures", modern missiology should learn from and highlight the strengths of every continent and country.[28] The hope is that this approach would have similar results for missiology and missions as a whole as it did for the city of Florence, which "became the epicenter of a creative explosion" and "one of the most innovative eras in history".[29] This is a *Medici Effect* for the Global Church, as it were. In a similar vein, Yeh later writes, "Diversity keeps us sharp as we engage with other Christian points of view, but it also keeps us humble if we truly listen to others who may correct any errors in our thinking."[30]

Implied in this concept of Polycentric Missiology is the assumption that, for polycentrism to be core to mission strategy, formation, and development, there needs to be polycentric leadership. A leadership that is more inclusive, communal, and collaborative becomes an important component as Polycentric Missiology continues to grow. This theory manifested itself in the way the 2010 congresses were planned. Ralph Winter, mission strategist and historian, originally had the idea for holding four congresses, which was further developed by his son-in-law Todd Johnson. At an important meeting in Boston that included the key leaders of each of these congresses, Johnson laid out the vision for these events as flowing from the Edinburgh Conference in 1910.[31] His rationale suggested that there should no longer be one center for mission in the world today. Rather, mission would be encompassed as a polycentric reality, streaming from everywhere to everywhere rather than having a central hub from which everything would flow.

---

[26] Yeh, 2016, 28.
[27] Yeh, 2016, 33.
[28] Yeh, 2016, 38.
[29] Yeh, 2016, 38.
[30] Yeh, 2016, 59.
[31] Yeh, 2015.

With this in mind Yeh shared the unique contribution of each of the congresses held in 2010 as well as the one in 2012. Tokyo 2010, for example, occurred as a result of this polycentric reality and was influenced primarily by Winter and his followers, who were mostly connected to the AD2000 and Beyond Movement, the US Center for World Mission, and Transform World. Consequently, it was the most evangelical and mission society-centered of the four events held that year. The primary product of the gathering was the Tokyo Declaration, which focused on finishing the task of making disciples of all nations. [32] From Yeh's perspective, "The Tokyo Declaration is multidimensional and stands as a much-needed corrective to some current missiological trends which have lost sight of the ultimate goal of mission, which is to bring the *panta ta ethne* [every people or ethnic group] into the worship of God."[33] Of course, a Polycentric Missiology and theology will likely reveal other perspectives in this as well.

Edinburgh 2010 may have been the most ecumenical of the four congresses and was lauded for its diversity. Although it was the smallest of the four events, the interactions were profound, the conversations and papers appeared more engaging, and ample time was provided for the participants to deeply engage.[34] Edinburgh 2010 produced the document *The Common Call*, which provided an ecumenical focus on those elements of Christian mission and biblical witness which unite the church worldwide.[35] The Listening Group report (a summary of the learnings from the conference) stated the strength of this mutual witness in these words:

> Many voices and narratives from different regional, confessional and other perspectives were heard at Edinburgh 2010. Arguments were articulated in an organic rather than a linear way and the conference appeared to us more as an event than offering a set of conclusions. Nevertheless, it was a time for thinking together and doing missional theology in a new and different way, expressing itself in the concluding *The Common Call*.[36]

2010Boston focused mostly on the student movement, building on John Mott's vision for the original Student Volunteer Movement.[37] It addressed the historic tensions of the tug-of-war between evangelism and social action. The strongest call at 2010Boston provided a prophetic critique, challenging the

[32] *Tokyo Declaration*, May 14, 2010.
[33] Yeh, 2010, 117.
[34] Yeh, 2010, 120-121.
[35] *The Common Call*, Scotland Assembly Hall, Edinburgh, June 6, 2010.
[36] *The Common Call*, 2010, 10.
[37] Yeh, 2015.

church's worldwide mission to repent for her neglect of dealing with core global issues.[38] ?

Cape Town 2010's primary contribution was that it was the largest, and perhaps most influential and enduring, of the four events that year. It had the distinction of being the most diverse gathering of church and mission leaders in history. It also highlighted a number of key global issues that need to be addressed. Those issues also arise in the *Cape Town Commitment*, a document from the Congress identifying the most pressing issues for mission in the coming years.

In a perceptive analysis of three of the four events held in 2010 (Edinburgh 2010, Tokyo 2010, and Cape Town 2010), Knud Jørgensen notes their similar characteristics:

> The inheritance from Edinburgh 1910 is at least: *World evangelization, making disciples, and a vision about mission and unity.* Before we look at how the three events handled this inheritance, it is, however, noteworthy that they all share the *Missio Dei* paradigm: mission begins with God and belongs to God ... the *Missio Dei* concept helped church and mission rethink and reinvent mission. In the course of the last decade or so most churches and movements have embraced it. The fact that it undergirds all three events – Edinburgh, Tokyo, and Cape Town is a strong indication that the starting point for their understanding of mission is the same.[39]

Similarly, mission historians Kenneth Ross and David Kerr stated, "Though in strictly institutional terms it is the World Council of Churches that is the heir of Edinburgh 1910, in terms of promoting the agenda of world evangelization, the Lausanne Movement might be seen as standing in direct continuity."[40] In addition, renowned mission scholar Andrew Walls proposed: "Both 'ecumenical' and 'evangelical' today have their roots in Edinburgh 1910. If each will go back to the pit whence both were dug, each may understand both themselves and the other better."[41]

CLADE V, considered the fifth significant congress highlighting the centenary, was held in Costa Rica in 2012 and was coordinated by the Fraternidad Teológica Latinoamericana (FTL), or the Latin American Theological Fellowship. This group was instrumental in informing and shaping the Lausanne Movement from the beginning, especially in terms of *misión integral,* or holistic mission. CLADE V highlighted this theme, offering

---

[38] Coon, Bradley A. and Gina A. Bellofatto. "Review of 2010 Boston: The Changing Contours of World Mission and Christianity," *MissioNexus,* 2011.

[39] Jørgensen, Knud. "Edinburgh, Tokyo and Cape Town: Comparing and Contrasting on the way to 2010." In Dahle, Margunn and Dahle, Lars along with Knud Jørgensen, eds., *The Lausanne Movement: A Range of Perspectives,* Oxford: Regnum, 2014, 356.

[40] Ross, Kenneth, and David Kerr. "The Commissions after a Century," in *Edinburgh 2010: Mission Then and Now.* Oxford: Regnum Books, 2009, 315.

[41] Ross and Kerr, 315.

a critique of the colonial approaches of other gatherings.[42] The leaders of the other congresses celebrating the centenary were by and large Western (or even if they were from other countries, a significant portion of their lives and education were from the West). CLADE stood alone among these five congresses for having indigenous Global South leadership and planning.[43]

Yeh concludes his book by advocating for Polycentric Missiology, suggesting that all of the congresses and their respective leaders point to a less centralized era of mission. In 1910, there was one congress and one hero who led the way. In today's modern, multipolar world, no one central event, leader, network, or movement can capture the whole picture. Yeh argues that we are now in an era of polycentrism:

> Which one of these five conferences did the best job of following Edinburgh 1910, a hundred years later? Which is worthy to be dubbed the true successor? The answer and the thesis of the book is that all of them are needed, and together they are the successor to Edinburgh 1910: no one conference or continent does mission best. But together, each provides a valuable piece of the puzzle.[44]

Mission today needs these voices. The perspectives from each continent and region are pivotal to reflecting the *Missio Dei*. The approaches from every sector of mission and society are critical for a better understanding and expression of World Christianity. Yeh goes further, suggesting:

> World Christianity is not just a momentary trend; it looks like it is here to stay. This includes every continent on earth, where every Christian can be mobilized to be a missionary to any land. This necessitates that we do mission differently, as the demographics of the world have changed drastically. We now live in an age of partnership, not paternalism, and V. S. Azariah's cry of "Give us friends!" from a century ago resounds in our ears and hearts as the Two-Thirds World churches have now come into their own.[45]

It is important to review the impact of Yeh's Polycentric Missiology and confirm his thesis that "this necessitates that we do mission differently".[46] We live in a world that reflects these truths and, in many ways, reacts to them. There is tension between the poles of globalism as advocated in places like France with Emmanuel Macron and Germany with Angela Merkel or the tribalism and nationalism that we see aggressively being pursued in India, through the *Hindutva,* and to a significant degree in the United States through America First. While these tensions continue to build, it is imperative that the Global Church rise above these factions and model a healthier approach.

---

[42] Yeh, 2016, 209-210.
[43] Note from Allen Yeh received on 21 October 2019.
[44] Yeh, 2016, 6.
[45] Yeh, 2016, 216.
[46] Yeh, 2016, 216.

Some might argue that Yeh's theory is naïve or simplistic given the complexities of our world and the challenge of threats like terrorism and irrational governments. Indeed, even the differences among each of the congresses could lead one to assume that no such unity is possible. That may well be the reaction by countries like the US or India, based on their fears of what the other might do or has done to them. While these do entail real concerns, the reality is that India still must negotiate with China and others for the good of their country. And while those in the US are more nationalistic currently, they still live in a world that requires engagement and continuing contact with other nations.

Other mission scholars have suggested that Yeh's research needs to go deeper. Scott Sunquist suggests that a more careful theological analysis would have been beneficial, but he assumes Yeh will be doing that in forthcoming research.[47] Kirsteen Kim provides a stronger assessment: "Let us build on [Yeh's] polycentric principles and have more missiological discussion from different centres. And let us collaborate for in-depth research so that we understand one another – and God's mission – all the better."[48] These critiques are helpful as they affirm Yeh's research while inviting continued research. Actually, some work does appear to augment Yeh's thesis. For example, Daryl Balia and Kirsteen Kim experimented with a polycentric missiological framework as they prepared for the Edinburgh 2010 conference, including voices from around the world that shared ideas in preparation for the conference. They drew attention to the polycentric structures in mission history, recognizing that polycentrism was prominent in the development of World Christianity.[49]

The questions flowing from these studies become: *In what ways does today's mission leader need to act differently than in eras past?* and *How do the highly varied contexts for mission require new forms of polycentric leadership?* This second question is what is reviewed in this study: the idea that there is an emerging form of leadership under a polycentric umbrella that is imperative for leading in a multipolar world. Yeh argues for a Polycentric Missiology that includes perspectives and wisdom from every corner of the world. While it may not be explicit, there does seem to be an implication here that polycentric mission structures, strategies, and development will require a new model of leadership that is collaborative and diverse and is seen through

---

[47] Sunquist, Scott. *International Bulletin of Mission Research* 41(4) 2017, 376-377.
[48] Kim, Kirsteen. Book Review, *Themelios*, 42 (2), 2017.
[49] Balia, Daryl M. and Kirsteen Kim. *2010. Witnessing to Christ Today*. Oxford: Regnum, 2010, 165-166. Also, Yeh importantly highlighted the distinction here in a follow up note: "I think this is an interesting distinction. Not that my idea is incompatible with Balia and Kim, but they are saying that international conferences ought to be organized with diverse leadership, but I am talking about multiple local conferences organized by indigenous leadership who eventually talk to each other." – correspondence on Feb 14, 2020.

local lenses, where each region of the world, and every country in those regions, is leading the way. Their only center is that of faith in Christ and the centrality of scripture. Thus, local and regional leadership and mission may look different, but all can inform the global expressions of mission.

This idea of Polycentric Missiology appears to be generating momentum. The recent Mission Commission Consultation for the World Evangelical Alliance used this as their theme due to the prominence of changes in the world today and the way that groups like the Wycliffe Global Alliance are shifting. Mary Lederleitner shared this in her plenary address:

> Polycentric mission is a holistic perspective and strategy that values multiple centers of power and influence engaged in mission around the globe, and actively seeks collaboration with them in ways that address marginalization and prioritizes decision- making shaped by a growing number of diverse voices and perspectives.[50]

Also noting this shift is missiologist Lalsangkima Pachuau:

> If the 1910 World Missionary Conference in Edinburgh represents the high point of the modern missionary movement from the West to Asia, Edinburgh 2010 marks another high point, namely Christian missions from Asia, by Asians, in Asia and around the world. It is this new missionary movement that will set the stage for mission in the next one hundred years.[51]

While Polycentric Missiology is gaining momentum, it must be acknowledged that some of these patterns can still be expressed and experienced as top-down, from one area of the world to another. Several of my colleagues who serve in Asia share their frustrations with nearby neighbors who are repeating missiological mistakes in exporting their forms of mission and leadership as well. Thus, while Polycentric Missiology is growing, we must be aware of how to best harness abuses of power and influences that do not reflect the Kingdom of God in each society.

Toward a Trinitarian Approach to Leadership

Success for mission leaders hinges on dependence on God the Father, Jesus the Son, and the Holy Spirit. It is in this Trinitarian relationship that a polycentric model draws significance. God the Father sends the Son and Holy

---

[50] Lederleitner, Mary. "Plenary Address Polycentric Missiology: the 14th annual Global Consultation in Panama" – WEA Mission Commission: The 14th Global Consultation of the World Evangelical Alliance Mission Commission, October 3-7, 2016.
[51] Lalsingkima Pachuau. "Missionaries Sent and Received, Asia, 1910-2010." In Johnson, Todd and Kenneth Ross, *Atlas of Global Christianity*, Edinburgh: Edinburgh University Press, 2009, 268.

Spirit to lead using their own unique giftedness. Together, they form a triad of leadership operating in unity through their diversity. It is in this style that leaders draw their strength and wisdom, knowing that only in being connected to the vine will we bear fruit.[52]

Leonardo Boff suggests, "The Trinitarian vision produces a vision of a church that is more communion than hierarchy, more service than power, more circular than pyramidal, more loving embrace than bending the knee before authority."[53] Similarly, Lesslie Newbigin sees the Trinity as a general model for mission overall.[54] It is fascinating that Newbigin draws from Michael Polanyi as a core influence in his theology of mission, because it was Polanyi who first suggested the idea of a polycentric perspective.

It is also interesting that leadership conceptions are mostly plural within the biblical record, supporting a Trinitarian or more polycentric approach. For example, when Moses was charged to lead the people of Israel, God appointed his brother Aaron to accommodate for Moses' fears about public speaking.[55] Later, his father-in-law Jethro advised him to appoint other leaders to share the load in leading the people of Israel.[56] God appointed prophets or seers to serve as advisors alongside of the kings.[57] Saul had Samuel, David had Samuel and Nathan, and Solomon had Nathan. Even the Hebrew word referring to the "counsel of God" is plural in orientation.[58] Jumping to the New Testament, Jesus sent out his disciples in teams for mission.[59] Paul also often traveled in teams and encouraged teamwork in mission.[60] Finally, in the establishment of local churches, elders were assigned to lead their faith communities.[61] Beyond these forms of plural leadership, polycentrism comes into further expression as each local fellowship is led by local leadership. They are one in the body of Christ, but each displays their independence as local communities, leading the way for the expression of faith in their local context. Thus, the church in Antioch is distinct from the Galatian and Roman churches. At the same time,

---

[52] John 15.

[53] Boff, Leonardo. *Trinity and Society*. Maryknoll, NY: Orbis, 1988, 154.

[54] Newbigin, Lesslie. *The Open Secret: An Introduction to the Theology of Mission.* Rev ed. Grand Rapids, MI: Eerdmans, 1995, 29, 65.

[55] Exodus 4:10-17; 7:1.

[56] Exodus 18:1-27.

[57] As examples see Saul and Samuel: 1 Sam 8-31; 1 Chron 9-10; David and Samuel (and Nathan): 1 Sam 16-31, 2 Sam 1-24, 1 Kings 1-2, 1 Chron 11-29; Solomon and Nathan: 1 Kings 1-11, 2 Chron 1-9.

[58] dwøs, *sode;* from 3245; a session, i.e. company of persons (in close deliberation); by implication, intimacy, consultation, a secret: —assembly, counsel, inward, secret (counsel). – *Strong's Hebrew and Chaldee Dictionary of the Old Testament*. Node 5475.

[59] Luke 10 and Mark 6.

[60] Pillette, Bard., "Paul and his Fellow Workers." *Emmaus*, 6, 1, 1996, 119-128.

[61] See Acts 14:23, Titus 1:5.

they are all part of the broader church and the body of Christ. These examples from scripture reveal a polycentric leadership model.

Len Hjalmarson suggests, "Trinitarian leadership is mutual, vulnerable, joyful, and loving, a dance at once mysterious and filled with purpose. Moreover, it is genuinely participatory: we partner with God in his ongoing mission in the world."[62] He says the approach rejects hierarchy, pointing to Jesus' teaching from Mark 10 where "the greatest of you must be the servant of all" to build on the New Testament teaching about the priesthood of all believers.[63] The idea is enhanced by Paul Stephens through the dynamic leadership relationship within the Trinity: *[handwritten: PLENTY OF SCRIPTURE THAT AFFIRMS HIERARCHY]*

> The Father creates, providentially sustains, and forms a covenantal framework for all existence. The Son incarnates, mediates, transfigures and redeems. The Spirit empowers and fills with God's own presence. But each shares in the other – coinheres, interpenetrates, cooperates – so that it is theologically inappropriate to stereotype the ministry of any one.[64]

Strengthening the approach is Milan Homola, who offers a Trinitarian leadership model in arguing against the commodification of the modern church and its approach to leadership. He builds on the participatory idea from Hjalmarson, suggesting that the Trinity operates communally: "The God who bestows his image upon creation is not an isolated individual, but rather exists communally."[65]

Dwight Zscheile states, "While the Trinity as a doctrine nearly ceased to function in the life of the Western church for several centuries in the modern period, retrieving it holds rich promise for theologically re-conceptualizing religious leadership in the twenty-first century."[66] He reimagines leadership in light of the Trinity, arguing leadership should have the mission of reconciliation at its core, strive toward unity in diversity, and view the cross and servant leadership as paramount. Ultimately, Zscheile suggests that "Trinitarian leadership is fundamentally collaborative."[67] Building on the theology of Moltmann and Volf, he continues:

[handwritten margin note: YES, BUT IT'S LIKE ARGUING FOR CLEAN AIR NO ONE DISAGREES ON THE END, JUST THE MEANS]

> Leadership communities in the image of the Trinity embrace a level of mutuality, reciprocal acknowledgement of each other's gifts, vulnerability to one another, and genuine shared life that transcends simply getting the job done. Thus

---

[62] Hjalmarson, Len. "The Trinitarian Nature of Leadership." *Crucible Theology and Ministry* 5:2, November 2013, 16.

[63] Hjalmarson, 10.

[64] Stevens, R. Paul. *The Other Six Days.*" Grand Rapids, MI: Eerdmans, 1999, 57.

[65] Homola, Milan "Unitarian Relational Leadership: The Myth!" 2008, 5. He draws on John 17, Genesis 1:26, and even Job 34:19.

[66] Zscheile, Dwight. "The Trinity, Leadership and Power." *Journal of Religious Leadership,* 6, 2, Fall, 2007, 43.

[67] Zscheile, 2007, 52-55.

cultivating a community in the image of the divine community – a community of reconciliation, interdependence, mutuality, difference, and openness – becomes central to leadership in a Trinitarian perspective. This includes both the community *of* leaders and the community *led* by the leaders.[68]

As we will discover, Zscheile highlights most of the themes discovered in my research towards a Polycentric Mission Leadership model.

Conclusion

Given what is seen both in Yeh's thesis about Polycentric Missiology as well as the findings from the Munich School on World Christianity and several other examples, we must grapple with the idea of polycentrism beyond merely the missiological and historical material. As we conclude this chapter, Yeh makes a plausible case that other scholars suggest deserve further study. And while there may be some who counter what is being learned through the Munich School, their research is solid and is filled with examples of polycentric development.

One tangible expression of polycentric leadership was discovered in the *festschrift* to Tite Tiénou mentioned above.[69] Caleb Oladipo, in looking at elements of mission history in Nigeria, described how Southern Nigerian Christian business leaders were key to establishing a Baptist Church movement in the North, a predominantly Muslim area of the country.[70] Westerners were blocked from working in the region, but national Nigerians could work there. The Southern Nigerians worked with other regional networks of believers, helping found the Baptist movement, so that today there is a Christian presence in the north because of this polycentric expression from mission history. It is, of course, not the whole story for Nigeria, but it does highlight a model that can be found throughout mission history as the Munich School so ably uncovers. So, while most of this chapter outlines the underpinnings of polycentrism and the need for a Polycentric Mission Leadership model, here is an example of the type of leadership necessary to bring about mission expansion.

This example portends what this study seeks to reveal: a new theoretical model for mission leadership is necessary. The next chapter explores emerging structures in governance, mission models, and local church expressions which become fertile soil for case studies to showcase a new theoretical approach to mission leadership.

---

[68] Zscheile, 2007, 57.

[69] Essamuah, Casely B. and David K. Ngaruiya, eds., *Communities of Faith in Africa and the African Diaspora: In Honor of Dr. Tite Tiénou with Additional Essays on World Christianity.* Eugene, OR: Wipf & Stock, 2013.

[70] Oladipo, Caleb O. "How Indigenous Traders Brought Christianity to Northern Nigeria," in Essamuah and Ngaruiya, 2013, 180-195.

3. Polycentric Structures and Governance

Introduction

As the mission movement has shifted in a more polycentric direction, there have been key developments in the theories underpinning church and mission organizations. Secular forms of leadership and corporate governance have had significant influence on church and mission structures. J.R. Woodward first applied polycentric thinking to church structures, arguing that the old hierarchical model with a pastor at the head reporting to a church board has become less effective as modernity has given way to postmodernity. Kirk Franklin channeled the same thinking into an incisive analysis of the merits of a polycentric model of leadership for the Wycliffe Global Alliance. Together, these are examples of how polycentric structures are changing the way we think about how churches and missions should run in practice.

Polycentrism (or "polycentricity") has also played a major influence in the political economy and in its management. Economist Elinor Ostrom won the Nobel Prize in Economics in 2009 for her work on polycentric governance, and over her career spawned an entire school of political economy at Indiana University – the Bloomington School. Ostrom's theoretical contribution and the surrounding body of work from the Bloomington School at Indiana University provide the theoretical framework for a polycentric model of leadership. [1] But the framework is only useful if it reflects the actual characteristics of modern leaders. The GLOBE study was a survey of CEOs and top management teams in 24 countries that gave a clear picture of what business leadership is like in the era of globalization. The evidence from the GLOBE study dovetails with the research on polycentric governance to create a strong foundation for a polycentric model of leadership. [2]

As we will see below, polycentric structures in churches and through mission contexts, combined with the evidence from polycentric governance, Movement Theory, and the GLOBE study on leadership, make a compelling case for an emergent theoretical model of Polycentric Mission Leadership. Building on the historical antecedents in the previous chapter, the models from these structures, when looked at through the lens of governance and movement theories, begin to lay out key thematic elements that we will develop in Chapter 4. These themes, or traits, as some might label them, find further

---

[1] Ostrom, 2010, 641-72.
[2] House, Dorfman, Javidian, Hanges, and Sully de Luque, 2014.

relevance when compared alongside the GLOBE study done across multiple cultures.

Polycentric Structures

J.R. Woodward, in his book *Creating a Missional Structure,* advocates for change within the church for postmodern society.[3] Writing from a North American context, he pinpoints one of the problems for the church being its hierarchical modern structures. He states:

> One of the reasons the church is losing the digital generation is we have failed to incarnate an approach to leadership which takes seriously the major shifts our culture is experiencing. If we are going to be a sign, foretaste, and instrument of God's kingdom and incarnate the good news in our context, we must learn to navigate the megashifts ... the media shift from print and broadcast to the digital age, the philosophical shift from modernity to postmodernity, the science shift from classic science to emergent science, the spatial shift from rural to urban, and the religion shift from Christendom to post-Christendom. These cultural shifts highlight the vulnerabilities of a centralized leadership structure, which I contend never should have characterized the church in the first place. If we are to meaningfully connect with the digital generation and live more faithfully to the narrative of Scripture, we need to shift from a hierarchical to a polycentric approach to leadership, where equippers live as cultural architects cultivating a fruitful missional ethos that fully activates the priesthood of all believers.[4]

He reasons that the current hierarchical leadership structure is ill-equipped to manage the challenges in society. Woodward's assessment of societal changes matches with *Global Trends 2030 – Citizens in an Interconnected and Polycentric World:* "The world is undergoing a massive transition, particularly in terms of power, demographics, climate, urbanization, and technology. In this context, the opportunities are huge, but so are the uncertainties and challenges to the well-being of citizens."[5]

Theologically, however, one might also look to passages like Matthew 9 (see v. 17), Mark 2 (v. 22), and Luke 5 (see vv. 37, 38). Jesus uses the metaphor of new wineskins, which could in some ways convey the need for adapting to different cultural contexts. Paul's words in 1 Corinthians 9 about adapting to local contexts might be applied conceptually as well. Normally, these passages

---

[3] Woodward, 2013.

[4] Woodward, 2013, 60.

[5] *Global Trends 2030 – Citizens in an Interconnected and Polycentric World report of the European Strategy and Policy Analysis System.* Institute for Security Studies European Union, Paris. It must be noted that futures-oriented publications are more predictive in nature rather than descriptive of current dynamics. It is important therefore, not to base new theory on more predictive analysis but maintain focus on discernable trends.

are interpreted for effectiveness in gospel witness, but they also augment Woodward's approach from Ephesians 4. Franklin suggests the Trinity in the *Missio Dei* as another theological justification for polycentrism in the next section.

Highlighting the type of environment that Woodward is addressing, Gen. Stanley McChrystal believes that "to succeed, maybe even to survive, in the new environment, organizations and leaders must fundamentally change. Efficiency, once the sole icon on the hill, must make room for adaptability in structures, processes, and mindsets that is often uncomfortable."[6] Leaders in these complex environments need to adapt and empower local teams to take more ownership of their own context. This can happen only if information is shared more broadly rather than held among a few at the top of the command chain.

This top-down, fixed-solution style of leadership was prominent in previous decades. Many leadership books of past eras highlight the role of the CEO, the pastor, or general manager.[7] McChrystal states that this type of leadership had strengths and weaknesses. On the positive side, it led to more products being produced in a faster time for less overall cost. For instance, companies like Ford Motor or US Steel maximized efficiency to manufacture products in record time, utilizing top-down management structures. However, "This new world [of conflict with Al-Qaeda] required a fundamental rewriting of the rules of the game. In order to win, we would have to set aside many of the lessons that millennia of military procedure and a century of optimized efficiencies had taught us."[8] He goes on to add, "These events and actors were not only more interdependent than in previous wars; they were also faster. The environment was not just complicated, it was complex."[9]

Woodward seems to capture the challenges of this new era. He sees the complexity of the world around him and notes, just as McChrystal did for the US military, that changes must take place in order for churches to be more effective. Before positing what new type of leadership might be necessary, he considers a biblical paradigm for leadership in the Early Church. He suggests Ephesians 4:7-16 as a model for ideal church structure and posits that this model would be more fruitful for today's environment. The Apostle Paul's five-fold pattern of leadership is a fluid structure where people with differing gifts lead at various times. Woodward notes how "[Paul] describes how Christ has given the church five different equippers – apostles, prophets, evangelists,

---

[6] McChrystal, Stanley, David Silverman, Tantum Collins, Chris Fusell. *Team of Teams: New Rules of Engagement for a Complex World*. New York: Penguin, 2015, 7.

[7] As examples: Iaoccoca, Lee. *Talking Straight*. London: Bantam, 1998; Welch, Jack. *Jack: Straight from the Gut.* London: Headline, 2005.

[8] McChrystal, 2015, 51.

[9] McChrystal, 2015, 59.

Who are these people in our modern context?

pastors, and teachers – who embody their gifts in such a way that the entire body is awakened and moves toward the full stature of Christ in both character and mission (Eph 4:7-16)."[10] Klyne Snodgrass affirms the importance of diversity in his commentary on this passage.[11] It's surprisingly similar to McChrystal's solutions in the fight against Al-Qaeda. For Woodward, this model of leadership from Ephesians forms the backbone of a polycentric leadership structure:

> The apostle Paul was ahead of his time, for he does not propose a centralized leadership structure or a flat leadership structure. Rather he reveals to us a polycentric structure, where leaders interrelate and incarnate the various purposes of Christ in such a way that the entire body is activated to service and matures in love. The five equippers are gifted by God to help the congregation move toward maturity in Christ and see the reality of God's kingdom, which is both here and coming.[12]

This is a model many church leaders are now advocating for, particularly in missional church leadership.[13] As highlighted in the previous chapter, the Trinity may serve as a model, but biblical history also lays out a more polycentric framework (see in particular 1 Corinthians 12:28, where various leadership gifts are detailed). [14] While Woodward's conception applies predominantly to diversity in leadership in local congregations, further studies in other structures uncover other aspects of this polycentrism that are imperative. To isolate polycentrism to this particular framework would miss the overall theoretical landscape. We will look at these ideas throughout this book.

In looking at communal leadership, Suzanne Morse highlights the importance of polycentric leadership as well:

> Successful communities, even those with long traditions of organized community leadership, will continue to broaden the circles of leadership to create a system for the community that is neither centralized nor decentralized, but

---

[10] Woodward, 2013, 58.

[11] Snodgrass, Klyne. *Ephesians: The NIV Application Commentary*. Grand Rapids, MI: Zondervan, 1996, 301, 306.

[12] Woodward, 2013, 60.

[13] See for example Hirsch, Alan. *The Forgotten Ways: Reactivating the Missional Church*. Ada, MI: Brazos Press, 2007, 169-177. And note the references above for Neil Cole and Alan Roxburgh (footnote 5).

[14] See Garland, David. *1 Corinthians. Baker Exegetical Commentary on the New Testament*. Grand Rapids, MI: Baker Academic, 2003, 976-977.

rather polycentric. The polycentric view of community leadership assumes that there are many centers of leadership that interrelate.[15]

Her model gives further support to Woodward's theological conception. Woodward refers to Kester Brewin's assessment of leadership in the Church in *Signs of Emergence*. Brewin is certain that:

> Studies of self-organizing, emergent systems, in areas such as computing, biology, and economics, demonstrate the necessity for organizations to move from the top-down institutional approach to a bottom-up, adaptable network approach that can meet the challenges of our fast-changing culture.[16]

> In every area of life, it seems there are historically top-down organizations that are having to adapt and evolve; that have realized that the only way that they can survive is to transform themselves from … monolithic, flabby, grey institutions that do not and cannot respond to realities on the ground, into conjunctive, devolved, bottom-up, adaptable networks that are trim, agile, and flexible enough to face and meet the ever-changing challenges of the fast-moving post-Enlightenment world.[17]

The ideas presented here by church leaders are amplified by the research on Complexity Theory. From this basis, leadership studies are considering Adaptive Leadership paradigms as a model for the "knowledge era".[18] Ronald Heifetz coined this phrase referring to leadership as "the act of mobilizing a group of individuals to handle tough challenges".[19]

Woodward's and Brewin's insights establish a good foundation for polycentric governance, which I will further develop with insights from the Bloomington School. Woodward has articulated something that is paramount for this thesis – that a polycentric form of leadership may be more effective for the church today.

---

[15] Morse, Suzanne. "Five Building Blocks for Successful Leadership," in *The Community of the Future*, ed. Frances Hesselbein et al. San Francisco, CA: Jossey-Bass, 1998, 234.

[16] Woodward, 2013, 71.

[17] Woodward, 2013, 209. See Brewen, Kester. *Signs of Emergence: A Vision for Church That Is Organic/Networked/Decentralized/Bottom-up/Communal/Flexible {Always Evolving}*. Grand Rapids, MI: Baker, 2007.

[18] Uhl-Bien, Mary, Russ Marion and Bill McKelvey. "Complexity Leadership Theory: Shifting leadership from the industrial age to the knowledge era." *Leadership Quarterly* 18:4, August 2007, 298-318.

[19] Heifetz, R. A., Grashow, A., & Linsky, M. (2009). *The practice of adaptive leadership: Tools and tactics for changing your organization and the world*. Boston, MA: Harvard Business Press.

Woodward's study was amplified by Kirk Franklin, who reviewed polycentrism as a model for leadership within the Wycliffe Global Alliance.[20] As Franklin stepped into leadership, both with Wycliffe Australia and later with the Wycliffe Global Alliance, he was aware of the challenges before him, such as the changing landscape of mission, structures that deserved re-thinking, the rising Majority World mission force, and the global cultural shifts. Franklin explored significant shifts occurring in the world of leadership and how that might impact the way Wycliffe operates on an international level. Franklin began by noting:

> The research question explored in this thesis concerns how globalization affects the missional journey of the Wycliffe Global Alliance (WGA) and how this is influenced by paradigm shift theory applied to the *Missio Dei*.[21]

> Together, these contribute to a theoretical model for a new paradigm for global mission leadership.[22]

Initially, Franklin reviewed the idea of *Missio Dei* in both theological and missiological perspectives, determining the importance of a Trinitarian approach to mission and leadership. He concluded this section of research, noting:

> As Christendom declines, the deliberate empowering of the people of God for mission is giving birth to a new paradigm of "participatory leader". This model understands how the church's identity is found in participating in the triune God's mission. Missional leaders do not necessarily rely on a title for their authority and often operate through leadership teams where spiritual gifts are emphasized … since the triune God is the perfect embodiment of hope and the originator and source of mission, he calls and enables his people to be a community of the witness of his hope. Leadership-in-community then becomes a natural outworking of the ongoing expression of participating in God's mission.[23]

---

[20] Franklin, Kirk James. "A Paradigm for Global Mission Leadership: The Journey of the Wycliffe Global Alliance." Ph.D. thesis, University of Pretoria, 2016.

[21] Franklin details the development of Paradigm Shift Theory to Thomas Kuhn and later to Hans Küng. He describes the evolving nature of science (taken from Kuhn) and applied to theology by Küng. See Kuhn, T., 2012, *The Structure of Scientific Revolutions*, 50th anniversary edition. Chicago, Il: University of Chicago Press; Küng, H., *Theology for the Third Millennium*, New York: Anchor Books, 1988, 128-152. Also see Franklin, 2016, 51-57. Simply stated, Franklin refers to changing paradigms over time and in this case to God's mission in the world today.

[22] Franklin, 2016, v.

[23] Franklin, Kirk J., Dave Crough, and Deborah Crough. *Towards Global Missional Leadership: A Journey Through Leadership Paradigm Shift in the Mission of God*. Oxford: Regnum, 2017, 597, 612.

Franklin's theological thesis is interesting, especially in light of mission leadership. He posits that the very nature of God, being Trinitarian, is an example of polycentric leadership: three distinct Persons leading based on their nature as one. This "leadership-in-community" concept is what he highlights as an important aspect of the *Missio Dei* – and he sees this model as instructive for a postmodern, plural world.

From this theological base, Franklin gives an overview of the benefits and challenges of globalization, some of which were highlighted above by Woodward. Franklin notes how globalization benefits societies because of "the intensification of worldwide social relations that link distant communities in such a way that local happenings are shaped by events occurring many miles away and vice versa."[24] On the other hand, "The very nature of globalization is contradictory – it creates winners and at the same time losers."[25] There are also economic disparities and polarization as nations go from pluralism on the one hand to tribalism on the other. This all leads toward greater nationalism which can manifest itself in both cultural and religious ways.

Clearly, globalization is something our world is grappling with in the present era. It is apparent in the UK's Brexit challenge with both "Remainers" and "Brexiters" arguing for their perspective as well as the America First principles affecting the United States. The challenge of increasing immigration and how the various EU countries are responding or the way that China's "Belt and Road" initiative is being thrust upon Asia are further examples. The poles between tribalism and globalism are ever before us. [26] From this context, Paul Bendor-Samuel, executive director of the Oxford Centre for Mission Studies, reflected on a gathering of mission agencies that came to this same conclusion: the need for a new type of leader. He suggested, "There is an urgent need for the development of global missional leaders who are able to make sense of our times and are capable of understanding and leading locally."[27]

With this backdrop, Franklin led Wycliffe on a journey involving a paradigm shift in how they do leadership. He invited leaders from across the Wycliffe community from the Global South and North to pursue a new way forward. It was in this context that Franklin used what he called a *Paradigm Shift Theory*, a model that adapts to the time period in which one operates, to move toward a polycentric approach toward governance. In the published book following his dissertation, he states:

> Albert Einstein is attributed as saying that major problems or challenges we have do not get solved with the same level of thinking that created them. If Einstein is right, how do we look beyond our own strategies and structures to find solutions

---

[24] Franklin, Crough and Crough, 2017, 39.
[25] Franklin, Crough, and Crough, 2017, 91.
[26] Bendor-Samuel, Paul. "Foreword" in Franklin, Crough, and Crough. 2017, 11.
[27] Franklin, Crough, and Crough, 2017, 12.

for the complexities of global mission? One way is to consider that the world has many centres of missional influence.[28]

Franklin's study is a fascinating, but eclectic, approach. He combines various streams of thinking via several approaches to analyze a number of factors present for mission leaders today. His work spans missional church paradigms, globalization, Paradigm Shift Theory, and the journey of the Wycliffe Global Alliance. Of utmost interest to us is a concept he summarizes as part of this span of research: the idea of polycentrism. Franklin states:

> A concept that is helpful in discussing the paradigmatic change in WGA is the concept of polycentrism, which is associated with or an outcome of globalization. This is because globalization … is the multidimensional social process and interconnection that multiplies and intensifies social interactions. It links these together in such a way that local developments in one part of the globe are affected by events in some other part of the world. It, therefore, creates an interconnected world made possible through widespread access to innovating and converging technologies, combined with economic and political influences, to produce dynamic forces not bound to a particular geographic or cultural context. Into this milieu arises the concept of multiple, or polycentric[,] centres of influence and leadership.[29]

He also looks at polycentrism through the prism of nation states and how they govern themselves. He leans heavily on Nadine Cattan's study of European governance, noting how cities located near each other form systems of leadership that strengthen one another and operate in a highly democratic and decentralized manner.[30] Borrowing from Cattan's model, Franklin explains how the Wycliffe Global Alliance can serve in a more empowering way: "polycentrism [has] implications for WGA's governance and structure because, as a global alliance, WGA inspires the interdependent self-governing organizations that make up WGA to collaborate together as a community, but retain their individual distinctions."[31] Later, he also notes:

> In a similar way, the polycentric approach of the dispersion of power is observed in the development of the new alliance structure of WGA. This has enabled the voices from the global South and East to take greater prominence in the governance and leadership of WGA."[32]

---

[28] Franklin, Crough, and Crough, 2017, 85.
[29] Franklin, 2016, 232.
[30] Cattan, Nadine. *Cities and Networks in Europe: A Critical Approach to Polycentrism.* Esher: John Libby Eurotext, 2007, 65-74.
[31] Franklin, Crough, and Crough, 2017, 233.
[32] Franklin, Crough, and Crough, 2017, 234.

Another aspect of polycentrism is found in the work of S.W. Morse in *The Community of the Future*. According to Morse:

> Effective communities broaden their sphere of leadership to form a polycentric model of numerous leadership centres that interconnect with each other. These centres enable the vision for the community through finding opportunities for its diverse array of people to make decisions, collaborate, and act together in suitable ways to reach the community's goal.[33]

Franklin expounds on this in his work looking at Gary Bowen[34] and Ron Hustedde,[35] stating:

> Bowen et al. suggest that informal and formal networks within a context operate like "turbines" that are not "centralized or pyramidal" in how they are governed but, instead, are polycentric with many interconnected centres of leadership. This provides "social energy" for building capacity in the community. Hustedde refers to this as an "entrepreneurial community", operating with a number of circles of influence, such as social services, youth, the arts, local government, and so forth. The leaders from each circle are enabled to make decisions directed by the mutual vision. Hustedde states that polycentric leadership works well when it moves beyond team building to 'team learning', where leaders think collectively and learn to work in a coordinated way.[36]

Franklin concludes:

> Polycentric leadership enables more of a communal approach in which leaders operate within an array of interconnected communities. Through polycentrism, there is a deliberate attempt to move away from established centres of power, so that one leads from among others. In this way, there is creative learning in a community, with attentiveness to others in the community, especially those from within the margins of the community.[37]

His observations have merit, but more research needs to be done to validate a polycentric leadership theory.

Franklin has built on Yeh's proposition and the findings of the Munich School to develop a polycentric model of leadership for the future. For Wycliffe, moving toward polycentrism has been positive. They have empowered previously unheard voices, given platforms to countries and

---

[33] Morse, S.W., 1998, 229-238.
[34] Bowen, G.L, Martin, J.A., Mancini, J.A. and Nelson, J.P. "Community Capacity: Antecedents and Consequences." *Journal of Community Capacity*, 8 (2), 1-21, 2000.
[35] Hustedde, R., 'What's culture got to do with it? Strategies for Strengthening Entrepreneurial Culture', in N. Walzer, *Entrepreneurship and Local Economic Development*. Plymouth: Lexington Books, 2007, 39-58.
[36] Franklin, Crough, and Crough, 2017, 235.
[37] Franklin, Crough, and Crough, 2017, 217.

regions that were formerly on the margins, gained further perspective from various centers of influence into the movement overall, and brought a dynamic sense of spiritual vitality and further missionary expansion. [38] This is something Jehu Hanciles predicts will become mission beyond the Christendom model:

> Mission de-linked from structures of power and domination; mission undertaken from positions of vulnerability and need; mission freed from the bane of territoriality and one-directional expansion from a fixed centre; mission involving agents who reflect the New Testament reference to the "weak things of the world" (1 Corinthians 1:27). [39]

In reviewing the Christendom model of church and mission, Hanciles sees the same challenges that Woodward and Franklin are seeking to address. In order for mission to thrive, it will need to adapt to new structures and approaches. This leads us to the ongoing research related to polycentric governance, which provides insight into better ways to lead in a polycentric fashion.

From the writings on church and mission structures, a number of themes arise. These include communal and collective focus, coordinated activity, empowerment, collaborative effort through teamwork, and the importance of diverse streams of input (similar to the Ephesians 5 gifts as well as multiple centers of influence). These themes come into further focus on the findings from the Bloomington School, which focus on polycentric governance.

Polycentric Governance

Paul Aligica and Vlad Tarko summarize the history of an emerging body of research into polycentric models of governance that arose out of the Bloomington School at Indiana University. Their definition of polycentricity was first envisaged by Michael Polanyi in *The Logic of Liberty*. [40] Polanyi considered polycentrism "as a social system of many decision centers having limited and autonomous prerogatives and operating under an overarching set of rules". [41] Aligica and Tarko go on to mention how these ideas have influenced studies in law, urban networks (which Franklin relied on heavily in his thesis), and, most importantly, in governance. This reached a peak when Elinor Ostrom received the Nobel Prize in Economics for her research. However, they note that "although the concept is often recognized as

---

[38] Franklin, Crough, and Crough, 2017, 242.

[39] Hanciles, Jehu J. 2008, 369.

[40] Polanyi, Michael. *The Logic of Liberty*. London: International Library of Sociology, 2013.

[41] Aligica, Paul D. and Vlad Tarko. *Governance: An International Journal of Policy, Administration, and Institutions*, 25, 2, April, 2012, 1.

important, not much has been done to further clarify and elaborate it, beyond the work of the aforementioned authors".[42] That is why further work is needed to bolster the argument for a theory, and my thesis is only the second attempt to look at polycentricity for the world of mission leadership.

Aligica and Tarko note, "Polanyi argued that the success of science was mainly due to its 'polycentric organization'. In such organizational systems, participants enjoy the freedom to make individual and personal contributions, and to structure their research activities in the best way they considered fit."[43] This concept is what the Bloomington School built upon in their studies and which Franklin used as the base for his missional leadership approach for the Wycliffe Global Alliance. The Bloomington School reviewed best practices for governing across various cities, states, and industries, leading to their proposals related to polycentric governance. Meanwhile, Franklin reviewed leadership across various countries and continents within the world of Wycliffe. The research from these two ideological streams supports the emergence of a polycentric theoretical model for mission leadership.

Elinor Ostrom, in her Nobel speech, shared how she, her husband, and other researchers, "introduced the concept of polycentricity in their effort to understand whether the activities of a diverse array of public and private agencies engaged in providing and producing public services in metropolitan areas was [sic] chaotic, as charged by other scholars – or potentially a productive arrangement".[44] Insightfully, their research draws attention to an important aspect of leading in an increasingly complex, global society:

> "Polycentric" connotes many centers of decision making that are formally independent of each other. Whether they actually function independently or instead constitute an interdependent system of relations, is an empirical question in particular cases. To the extent that they take each other into account in competitive relationships, enter into various contractual and cooperative undertakings or have recourse to central mechanisms to resolve conflicts, the various political jurisdictions in a metropolitan area may function in a coherent manner with consistent and predictable patterns of interacting behavior. To the extent that this is so, they may be said to function as a "system".[45]

Throughout her lecture, she cites her own studies in water management as well as others' studies of policing, forestry, and farming, highlighting the efficiencies of a polycentric form of authority and decision making. She found that "when subjects communicate face-to-face, they frequently agree on joint strategies and keep to their agreements – substantially increasing their net returns. Further, communication to decide on and design a sanctioning system

---

[42] Aligica and Tarko, 2012, 1.
[43] Aligica and Tarko, 2012, 2.
[44] Ostrom, 2010, 411.
[45] Ostrom, 2010, 411.

enables those choosing this option to achieve close to optimal returns."[46] This governance through community highlights a set of practices that supplement the emerging idea for polycentric leadership. René Brohm suggests:

> Polycentric order is a social order without one dominant center, but with different centers that exercise varying amounts of power depending on the issue at stake. The particularity of this kind of organizing is that it uses the tensions arising from a diversity of perspectives in a group of people. It is possible to organize and at the same time allow for different understandings and perspectives.[47]

Refining even further, he notes, "Polycentric order was thus characterized in terms of perspectivity and participation. Shared perspectives and collective practices constitute polycentric order. These emerge from shared participation."[48]

The idea of having multiple centers of influence working together for better collective ideation and decision making seems to have merit. What Yeh and the Munich School have mined, and what Woodward posits and Franklin explores, seem to have theoretical coherence. The question is: *Does this concept have further data to support its development?*

Brohm tests out this theory in a business to see how people function within a large, complex industry, highlighting how people from different sectors of the business synergize from their different ecosystems when they work together by bringing new ideas to one another, strengthening the work of the overall company.[49] He concludes:

> Some catalysts of meaning reinforce each other to develop shared interpretative tendencies and collective performances. These tendencies and performances create one side of the interface. Mutual adjustments between groups then means that particular catalysts of meaning become destabilized and need to be tacitly repaired or collectively renegotiated. Coherence in such a polycentric order develops on the basis of the interconnections between the different interfaces through catalysts of meaning.[50]

In essence, Brohm's research implies there is some validity to the use of a polycentric model of governing – at least within the ecosystem of this particular company.

---

[46] Ostrom, 2010, 425.
[47] Brohm, René. *Polycentric Order in Organizations: a dialogue between Michael Polanyi and IT-consultants on knowledge, morality, and organization.* Rotterdam: Erasmus University, 2005, 36-37.
[48] Brohm, 2005, 42.
[49] Brohm, 2005, 171.
[50] Brohm, 2005, 173.

Looking at polycentrism from a political perspective, Jan Aart Scholte emphasizes how interactions across nation states have become more collective in governance:

> Governance in the more global world of the twenty-first century has become distinctly multi-layered and cross-cutting. Regulation occurs at – and through interconnections among – municipal, provincial, national, regional and global sites. No single "level" reigns over the others, as occurred with the primacy of the state over suprastate and substate spheres in territorialist circumstances. Instead, governance tends to be diffuse, emanating from multiple locales at once, with points and lines of authority that are not always clear."[51]

> "it is plain that globalization has significantly affected the mode of governance. In tandem with this reconfiguration of social space, the statist mould of old has given way to a polycentric framework. States continue to figure very significantly in this post-statist condition, but they are embedded in multilayered and diffuse networks of regulation. Polycentric governance occurs through diverse and often interconnected public and private arrangements on varying scales from local to global. The situation has lacked a clear centre of command and control of the sort that the Westphalian sovereign state once provided.[52]

Here again, we have another premise showing how governance operates in a more polycentric manner. Globalization has led the nations of the world to operate in a much more dynamic fashion, interacting with one another at various levels. Even in today's age of disruption and the consistent arguments against globalism, the reality is that governments must interact with one another in order to work out a better future.

In all of these studies, the pattern of effectiveness displayed through polycentric governing systems reinforces Franklin's premise in approaching the Wycliffe Global Alliance. A polycentric leadership paradigm fits an era when global interaction and multipolar decision making is not only helpful, but critical. What Yeh discerned for missiology and what the Munich School discovered in mission history appear to be pointing us to the future of leadership. Certainly, the Bloomington School has made significant progress when it comes to researching polycentric governance.

An important component of the governance research identified common themes that are also in the Polycentric Mission Leadership model and will be addressed in relation to the Lausanne Movement later. One of the themes that appears is freedom – operating within one's own group or structure, working together across a diverse array of centers of decision making, or working in cooperative or contractual relationships using shared perspectives and

---

[51] Scholte, Jan Aart. "Globalization and Governance: From Statism to Polycentrism." In *Globalization: A Critical Introduction*. London: Red Globe Press, 2004, 3.
[52] Scholte, 2004, 42.

collective processes. These collaborative endeavors operate in a multilayered fashion through interdependent connections that flow from a diverse array of people and places.

GLOBE Study

The GLOBE study gives further credibility to the research on polycentrism through their focus on global leadership for business leaders. The first of these projects was a ten-year quantitative survey of global managers in 62 societies.[53] The findings from that study were supplemented in a country-by-country study from 25 countries, which further strengthened the results.[54] These studies highlighted what may be the first verifiable set of data on cross-cultural leadership traits for business leaders. It's important to note that the rubric of success for those in business is based primarily on profit, whereas success for NGOs and missions is based on fulfilling their mission. Even with this variation, the traits found among business leaders in the GLOBE study do have substantive crossover for NGOs, churches, and mission organizations.

It was particularly interesting to review CEO behavior in light of those findings.[55] There are intriguing parallels to polycentric leadership.

The authors in the study noted that "the 20-year-long Global Leadership and Organizational Behavior Effectiveness (GLOBE) Research Program set the goal of empirically determining the role of culture in leadership behavior and effectiveness. It contributed to building evidence-based managerial and leadership theories and practices."[56] The study established that leaders are most effective when they are charismatic, team-oriented, and humane.[57]

From the research, they built on the foundation of Implicit Leadership Theory (ILT)[58] and Culturally endorsed Implicit Leadership Theory (CLT)[59] to present a theoretical framework linking national culture, organizational culture, and leadership.[60] ILT proposes that people have preconceived notions of how the world operates and they behave based on how they interpret and

---

[53] House, Robert and Paul Hanges, Mansour Javidian, Peter Dorfmann and Peter Gupta. *Culture, Leadership, and Organizations: The GLOBE Study of 62 Societies.* Thousand Oaks, CA: Sage, 2004.

[54] House, Robert and Jagdeep Chhokar and Felix Broadbeck. *Culture and Leadership Across the World: The GLOBE Book of In-Depth Studies of 25 Societies.* London: Psychology Press, 2007.

[55] House, Hanges, Javidian, Dorfmann and Sulley du Luque. 2014.

[56] House, 2014, xv.

[57] House, 2014, xvi.

[58] See Lord, R.G. and Maher, K.J. "Alternative information processing models and their implication for theory, research, and practice." *Academy of Management Review,* 15(1), 1990, 9-28.

[59] Javidan, M. Teagarden, M., Bowen, D. "Making it Overseas." *Harvard Business Review,* April, 2010, 109-115.

[60] House, 2014, 52.

respond to those in leadership.[61] Throughout the study, the authors point to CLT as a key part of their overall construct. They highlight six global leadership dimensions: charismatic/value-based, team-oriented, participative, humane-oriented, autonomous, and self-protective.[62]

Two of these traits – team-oriented and humane – dovetail with the findings from polycentric leadership. Another trait that didn't score as high – participative – would seemingly contradict the polycentric model, but when one looks deeper into the meaning of this attribute, it is still valid. In essence, the participatory trait was less apparent in more hierarchical cultures but still a strong attribute in most successful CEO behavior. Thus, its validity for polycentric leadership is still operable, just with less strength for the GLOBE study among hierarchical cultures.

The authors define the *charismatic* dimension as follows: "according to GLOBE 2004, Charismatic/Value-Based leadership includes the conventional attributes of vision, inspiration, and self-sacrifice. However, it goes beyond these attributes and includes three other important dimensions: integrity, decisiveness, and performance orientation."[63] Later in the book, they note that this particular dimension is the most determinative of leadership success,[64] yet they go out of their way to clarify how their definition is different from more popular interpretations (or conceptualizations):

> However, it is very important for us to point out that our view of Charismatic leadership is very different from the use of this term in the popular press. A charismatic leader has become synonymous with a leader who is flamboyant, showy, and captivating and who often exists within the political arena. For GLOBE, Charismatic leadership embodies the leadership characteristics of vision, inspiration, performance-oriented, decisive, and high integrity. This person may be exemplary but does not have to be superman nor exemplify a flashy and over-the-top demeanor. According to our criteria, both Bill Gates of Microsoft fame and Warren Buffett of Berkshire Hathaway qualify as outstanding charismatic leaders; neither is flashy and showy yet both embody many of the qualities found in the GLOBE Charismatic leadership behavior (i.e., visionary, performance-oriented, integrity, and decisive). Both have achieved success as business leaders and philanthropists but neither considers themselves [as being] charismatic.[65]

The second dimension critical to global leaders is being *team-oriented*, which leaders display through loyalty "to their teams and care for the welfare of their team members. They use their administrative and interpersonal skills to manage the team's internal dynamics and to create a cohesive working

---

[61] Lord and Maher, 1990, 9-28.
[62] House, 2014, 55.
[63] House, 2004, 58.
[64] House, 2004, 260.
[65] House, 2004, 268.

group."[66] The authors suggest that the "Team-Oriented leadership dimension includes the following primary leadership dimensions: (1) collaborative team orientation, (2) team integrator, (3) diplomatic, (4) malevolent (reverse scored),[67] and (5) administratively competent."[68] This attribute is clearly present in the polycentric leader. Additionally, they found that on the team-oriented scale:

> In contrast to the almost universal emphasis of transformational factors among all samples, team building stood out in the American and Southern European regions but much less so in the Far Eastern region. This finding presents an obvious paradox with respect to the highly individualistic American executives and collectivistic East. The authors speculated that it may be because of the emphasis on teamwork in the Far East that these executives failed to see (or mention) teamwork although it is an ingrained aspect of their work life. Perhaps akin to American individualism as a defining cultural factor, Americans are inveterate joiners of organizations and teams.[69]

Despite this divergence, later in the study, the effectiveness of a CEO across the spectrum relies heavily on this team-oriented feature. So, while *participatory* may not have scored high in the effectiveness metrics, and *team-oriented* did not show as much significance in the Far East, key polycentric leadership traits mentioned earlier like "collaborative team orientation", "team integrator", and "diplomatic" are still important to success. Thus, the participatory dimension may have had less to do with collaboration and working together as a team and more about simply the style of the leader.

The third high-scoring dimension, but not nearly as important as the previous two, is having a *humane orientation*, a trait that aligns with something I simply call *relational*. The GLOBE study defines humane orientation as having "empathy for others by giving time, money, resources, and assistance when needed. It reflects concern for followers' personal and group welfare."[70] This is where character traits like humility and modesty come into play. It is these very traits, especially empathy for others, sharing resources and time, and thinking of the group, that sync with polycentrism.

Overall, of the six attributes in the GLOBE study, "It is clear ... that across the countries in our sample, leaders are generally expected to be Charismatic, Team-Oriented, Participative, and somewhat Humane-Oriented. They are not expected to be Autonomous or Self-Protective."[71] Three of the top four

---

[66] House, 2004, 65.
[67] Malevolent refers to "leaders who are dishonest, vindictive, and deceitful and act negatively toward others" – See House, 2004, 65ff.
[68] House, 2004, 66.
[69] House, 2004, 68.
[70] House, 2004. 76.
[71] House, 2004, 210.

dimensions relate directly to the polycentric governance styles highlighted previously and, while the participative dimension doesn't always lead to outstanding results, it still comes out as one of the important aspects of global leadership.[72] For leaders to operate well within a polycentric system, they must be team-oriented, humane-oriented, and participatory. In the GLOBE study, the charismatic dimension came out as the top trait, yet it is defined quite differently than what is seen in more popular renditions of that concept. Perhaps related to this is their assessment:

> We found that CEOs do matter – and they matter greatly. Our results support the view in the literature that CEOs do have an impact on the performance of their firms. Using both internally oriented and externally oriented measures of performance, we found that CEO behavior is significantly correlated with firm performance.[73]

The GLOBE study discovered a set of traits marking the effectiveness of global business leaders who may operate in different spheres than leaders in the mission or church world, but who still share many of the same attributes.[74]

Common themes exist between the various studies that pinpoint key aspects of a Polycentric Mission Leadership model. Before detailing those themes more fully in the next two chapters, let's look at how Movement Theory, networks, and collaborative leadership also influence the conception of the polycentric model of leadership.

Movement Theory

Another helpful aspect in examining Polycentric Mission Leadership is to review Movement Theory, with a particular focus on religious (missional) and church movements. The research conducted by Theodore Esler on *Movements and Missionary Agencies* is insightful.[75] Esler provided an overview of various aspects of Movement Theory, looking at social, organizational, and religious movements and assessing various movement theories by focusing on resource

---

[72] It is important to note the differences between the profit end goal versus the goals of an NGO or mission in this instance. Part of the discrepancy in this study could be related to this profit perspective. That said, the GLOBE study still did find relevance for the participatory function for CEOs.

[73] House, 2004, 345.

[74] For an understanding of the value of various "traits" in leadership, see Northouse, 2013, 19ff.

[75] Esler, Theodore. 'Movements and Missionary Agencies: A Case Study of Church Planting Missionary Teams.' Fuller Seminary Dissertation, March, 2012.

mobilization. In the end, he proposes a "General Integrated Movement Attribute Model",[76] stating:

> Resource mobilization theory suggests that movement organization is a dominant feature of a movement. Evaluation of a movement must, therefore, include and broaden the scope of our study to include organizational culture. Understanding the missionary agency as an organization bent on forming religious movements opens up the possibility that organizational theory can be applied to the study of movements.[77]

Esler began by reviewing new social movements and social movement organizations and sought insights from these models and theories to better understand how church planting teams could be more effective. According to Herbert Blummer:

> Social movements can be viewed as collective enterprises seeking to establish a new order of life. They have their inception in a condition of unrest and derive their motive power on one hand from dissatisfaction with the current form of life, and on the other hand, from wishes and hopes of a new system of living. The career of a social movement depicts the emergence of a new order of life.[78]

These movements, Esler says, are much more like leading mission societies than traditional models of organizational leadership. The collective nature of their organization is what is so similar to leading in polycentric fashion.

Jehu Hanciles adds to this view, suggesting that movements are led by multiple leaders in a polycentric fashion. [79] The idea that leadership in flourishing movements is collaborative is pivotal to a new theoretical model for mission leadership. Many social movements depend on volunteer action and Edgar Schein highlights this in describing the nature of the movements and how volunteers organize around common interests. [80] Andrew Walls further points this out in relation to missionary movements. [81] As these volunteers organize themselves, at least in terms of movements, they do so, as Hanciles suggests, in polycentric fashion. Esler concludes, "Volunteer missionary societies are similar to the theorized 'social movement

---

[76] Esler defines resource mobilization as anything "that a movement needs in order to form and carry out its objectives. It might be people, money, identity, or other movement assets." 2012, 38.

[77] Esler, 2012, 65.

[78] Blumer, H. *Symbolic Interactionism: Perspective and Method.* Berkeley, CA: University of California Press, 1969, 99.

[79] Hanciles, 2009, 40-47.

[80] Schein, Edgar H. *Organizational Culture and Leadership.* San Francisco, CA: Jossey-Bass, 1985, 79.

[81] Walls, Andrew. *The Missionary Movement in Christian History: Studies in the Transmission of Faith,* Maryknoll, NY: Orbis Books, 1996, 80.

organization' which seek[s] to bring about a movement's goals by gaining a resource base."[82] Thus, voluntary action is important for leading social and mission movements. And, as Hanciles advocates, these movements hinge on a variety of leaders rather than one centralized leader.

While there is a great deal to learn from Social Movement Theory for leading missional movements, Esler rightly notes that religious movements don't necessarily form from a position of unrest.[83] William Sims Bainbridge describes these movements as follows:

> A religious movement is a relatively organized attempt by a number of people to cause or prevent change in a religious organization or in religious aspects of life. Religious movements have some similarities with political, cultural, and social movements, in that they are collective human attempts to create or to block change.[84]

The strength of Esler's research is in reviewing a variety of streams from mission and church history. Since he was interested in solidarity movements, he reviewed the works of missiologists such as Roland Allen, Donald McGavran, and David Garrison and was surprised at his findings about leadership, identifying a dichotomy. The observations mostly point to a multiplicity of leaders for a movement (see Hanciles' affirmation above), but Paul Pierson suggests that "breakthroughs, expansion, renewal movements and the like are almost always triggered by a key person".[85] Esler suggests that a possible reconciliation may be in the form of the leader purely as a "catalyst or lightning rod" rather than as the sole leader of the movement.[86]

David Hesselgrave takes the Social Movement Theory approach, suggesting that the role of the leader is not as important as the people within the movement.[87] This seems to resonate well with what we see on TED Talks that speak of the importance of the "First Follower",[88] a term Derek Sivers talks about in relation to the critical role the first follower plays in a movement getting started.

Steve Addison highlights in *Pioneering Movements: Leadership that Multiplies Disciples and Churches* the critical need for movement leadership:

---

[82] Esler, 2012, 84.
[83] Esler, 2012, 23.
[84] Bainbridge, William Sims. *The Sociology of Religious Movements*. New York: Routledge, 1997, 3.
[85] Pierson, *The Dynamics of Christian Mission*. Pasadena, CA: William Carey Library, 2009, 135-149.
[86] Esler, 2012, 52.
[87] Hesselgrave, David F., Donald McGavran, and Jeff Reed. *Planting Churches Cross-Culturally: North America and Beyond*. 2nd ed. Grand Rapids, MI: Baker Academic, 1978, 318.
[88] Sivers, D. *How to start a Movement*. TED Talk, YouTube, 2010.

For better or for worse, movements create and remake the world we live in. If we want to change the world, we must understand movements. In simple terms, a movement is a group of people committed to changing the world. The spheres of politics, science, culture, and faith are shaped and remade by movements.[89]

He then identifies five levels of leadership in a multiplying movement: seed sellers, church planters, church multipliers, multiplication trainers, and movement catalysts [90] describing these leaders as ones who start, build, multiply, train, and catalyze for the growth of the movement. Addison writes, "Their job is to 1) seed discontent with the status quo, 2) cast a vision of what God could do, and 3) provide simple but profound methods to get people started and help them remain on track."[91] His work on movement leaders is a combination of his own experience and anecdotal evidence from those he interviewed. His conclusion was that there were attributes common to polycentrism, namely freedom or entrepreneurialism. Polycentric missional leaders are entrepreneurs, which is an important aspect of leading mission movements.

Similar traits are discovered in Dave Logan's popular book *Tribal Leadership*. Logan suggests that there is synergy between the leader and his or her tribe or group. The stronger the bonds between them, the stronger the movement: "This is how Tribal Leadership works: the leader upgrades the tribe as the tribe embraces the leader. Tribes and leaders create each other."[92] This affirms Esler's research that the key to catalyzing movements is through resource mobilization, and this begins with the mobilization of people toward a common cause and builds as a community that forms around that cause. Logan developed another polycentric leadership theme found in my research: *communal*. The communal leader works within a community or collective in order to lead a movement well.

Esler also highlights the work of John L. Campbell in developing a *bricolage*[93] as a fresh way to form these cooperatives. These bricolages bring disparate forces together in ways that forms new social activities. Mayer Zald and Roberta Ash describe these types of coalitions: "The coalition pools resources and coordinates plans, while keeping distinct organizational

---

[89] Addison, Steve. *Pioneering Movement: Leadership that Multiplies Disciples and Churches*. Downers Grove: IVP Books, 2015, 15.

[90] Addison, 2015, 95.

[91] Addison, 2015, 141.

[92] Logan, Dave, John King, and Halee Fischer-Wright, *Tribal Leadership*. New York: Harper Collins, 14.

[93] Campbell defines 'bricolage' as "an innovative recombination of elements that constitutes a new way of configuring organizations, social movements, institutions, and other forms of social activity." Campbell, J. L. 2002. Where do We Stand? Common Mechanisms in Organizations and Social Movements Research. *Social Movements and Organization Theory Conference*, 9.

identities."[94] This idea, which is seen in the studies on governance earlier, shows the important theme of collaboration in operating to coordinate or shape movements. This further affirms the essence of polycentric leadership as a collaborative, collective form of leadership.

These same ideas from social movements are magnified when looking at network and collaborative leadership models. Kenneth Ross remarked on the significance of network leadership as a viable structure for mission movements compared to the structures during Edinburgh 1910:

> The structures for this new migratory mission movement differ from the mission societies of 1910. There is no head office, no organizing committee, no command structure, no centralized fund, and no comprehensive strategic direction. Rather than structures, people in the new movement talk about networking, requiring lesser [sic] resources. The emphasis is on relations and less on strategies.[95]

Network leadership is a model increasingly being studied for social movements because of its effectiveness for complex environments. Candace Jones, Hesterly, and Borgatti point this out in their research in cross-sector business environments. They highlight the importance of exchanges between sectors, which enable problem-solving that improves efficiency. They note how Japanese car manufacturers, using network models of exchange, have significantly improved time production compared to American carmakers. Core to their studies was the frequency of interactions between diverse sectors and talent.[96] The ongoing studies of social movements, especially in relation to organization studies, show promise since the models enhance community action.[97] Consensus and cooperation lead to collective action in communal leadership activity, particularly when trust is built between the parties.[98]

Social Movement theorist Edward Schein pinpoints another key component critical to polycentric leadership: *diversity.* Schein states:

> For diversity to be a resource ... the subculturals must be connected and must learn to value each other enough to learn something of each other's culture and

---

[94] See Zald, MN, and R Ash. "Social Movement Organizations: Growth, Decay and Change." *Social Forces,* 44 (3) 1966, 327-341. Also, Esler, 2012, 93-95.

[95] Ross, Kenneth. 'From Edinburgh 1910 to Edinburgh 2010', in Mogens Mogensen ed., 2009, 31.

[96] Jones, Candace, Hesterly and Borgatti. "A general theory of network governance: Exchange conditions and social mechanisms," *The Academy of Management Review,* 22, 1997, 911-945.

[97] Weber, Klaus and Brayden King. *Social Movement Theory and Organization Studies.* In *Oxford Handbook of Sociology, Social Theory and Organization Studies,* Paul Adler, Paul du Gay, Glenn Morgan, Mike Reed (eds.), 2013, 9-10.

[98] Schneider, Mark, John Scholz, Mark Lubell, Denisa Mindruta, and Matthew Edwardsen. "Building Consensual Institutions: Networks and the National Estuary Program," *American Journal of Political Science,* 47, 1, 2003, 152.

language. A central task for the learning leader, then, is to ensure good cross-cultural communication and understanding throughout the organization. Creating diversity does not mean letting diverse parts of the system run on their own without coordination. Laissez-faire leadership does not work, because it is in the nature of subgroups and subcultures to protect their own interests. To optimize diversity, therefore, requires some higher-order coordination mechanisms in mutual cultural understanding.[99]

Esler builds on Schien's call for cultural awareness, noting the need for cultural acumen to lead movements and structures well:

> In a bricolage organization, in which numerous cultures are cooperating for the same objective, the context becomes much more important. It is the very "richness" of this context that makes diversity desirable. It also may lead to insider-outsider dynamics because only those who understand the context are able to participate effectively.[100]

For a collaborative model to be most effective, diversity is an important element. And, when one looks at scripture, there is a unifying ideal that every tongue, tribe, and nation will worship in harmony.[101] This was foreshadowed in Acts 2, when people were speaking in languages that others could understand.[102] It is also reminiscent of the biblical unity pointed to in Galatians 3 and the call to be united no matter our differences.[103] Oscar Cullmann suggests in reflecting on 1 Corinthians 12 that, "the richness of the full measure of the Holy Spirit consists in ... plurality".[104]

Conclusion

The Nobel award-winning research by Elinor Ostrom gives initial credibility to a polycentric theoretical model, making a strong theoretical argument for this new approach. The findings from the Bloomington School over several decades lend both credence and refining characteristics to this emergent theory. Augmenting that research is the more recent GLOBE study findings, which supplement and refine the model and provide cross-cutting research to contrast and verify the core characteristics. Finally, the research on Movement

---

[99] Schein, 1985, 143-144.
[100] Esler, 2012, 220.
[101] Rev. 7:9-17.
[102] Acts 2:1-13.
[103] Gal. 3:26-29. See also the work of Oscar Cullmann, *Unity through Diversity: Its Foundation and a Contribution to the Discussion Concerning the Possibilities of Its Actualization*, trans. M. Eugene Boring. Minneapolis, MN: Fortress Press, 1987 and Stéphanie Dietrich. "God's Mission as a Call for Transforming Unity: Call for Transforming Unity," *International Review of Mission* 107(2): 378-390.
[104] Cullmann, 1987, 12.

Theory augments the research, lending further viability to a Polycentric Mission Leadership theoretical model.

The initial review of a few of these emergent models in structures of leadership reinforces and refines the findings. These models will be further amplified as we test the theory through using the Northouse approach to evaluating leadership theory in the next chapter.

Given the strength of these various approaches, the common traits point to an approach that is both promising and that has merit for mission leaders. Communal collaboration through relational networks operating in entrepreneurial frameworks and inspired by character-based charismatic leaders form many of the themes outlined in this polycentric theoretical model. Now we turn our attention to the actual model itself. Looking at these models of structure and governance, we are able to espouse a new theoretical model.

4. A Model of Polycentric Leadership

Introduction

This idea of a polycentric form of leadership is still nascent and mostly untested. The approach is building momentum though. As highlighted above, Mary Lederleitner highlighted its usefulness at a recent Mission Commission Consultation for the World Evangelical Alliance:

> Polycentric mission is a holistic perspective and strategy that values multiple centers of power and influence engaged in mission around the globe, and actively seeks collaboration with them in ways that address marginalization and prioritizes decision-making shaped by a growing number of diverse voices and perspectives.[1]

Lederleitner captures the potential of polycentricity. It values wisdom from multiple places of power and influence that builds collaboration to address challenges being faced. It uses a broader range of leaders and insights to improve mission strategy and implementation. In this insightful description she recognizes many of the key themes I identified for a new polycentric model of mission leadership.

Here I will describe each of these themes – collaborative, communal, diverse, free, relational, and charismatic – and then evaluate the new theoretical construct using the Northouse approach, which is a reliable framework for reviewing theoretical models in leadership studies[2] that is often cited as a common standard in academic research.[3] The approach goes into detail on the primary active theories around a subject and provides a depth of analysis that is rarely displayed in such a comprehensive manner.[4]

---

[1] Lederleitner, 2016.

[2] Northouse, 2013.

[3] Dinh, J. E., Lord, R. G., Gardner, W. L., Meuser, J. D., Liden, R. C., and Hu, J. "Leadership theory and research in the new millennium: Current theoretical trends and changing perspectives," *Leadership Quarterly*, 25 (1), 2014, 36-62.

[4] As an example of a more descriptive approach, yet one with substance and some comparative material, see Avolio, B. J., Walumbwa, F. O., and Weber, T. J. "Leadership: Current theories, research, and future directions." *Annual Review of Psychology*, 60, 2009, 421–449. Another more descriptive analysis can be seen in John Saee "Effective leadership for the global economy in the 21st century," *Journal of Business Economics and Management*, 6:1,2005, 3-11.

Polycentric Leadership Themes

The chart below provides a visual overview of the emergence of a polycentric model of leadership and the corresponding components to lead adeptly within this framework. By examining the crossover themes, a pattern emerges that forms the foundation for a new theoretical model on Polycentric Mission Leadership.

Table: Chart of Crossover Themes

Polycentric Structures	Polycentric Governance	GLOBE Study	Crossover or Common Themes
Collaboration/Network	Shared Participation/Collective Practice	Participative	Collaborative: Collaboration/Network/ Participative/Shared/Collective
Interconnected Communities Leadership in Community	Contractual or Cooperative Undertaking	Team-Oriented/ Team Work	Communal: Community/Contractual or Cooperative/ Own Ecosystem/Mutual Vision/Team
	Diversity of Perspective yet also Shared/ Cross-Cultural Capacity		Diverse: Diversity/Cross-Cultural
Entrepreneurial Community, Risk Taker, Experimentation, Innovation and Catalyst	Own Eco-System Freedom to Structure in Their Own Way Freedom of Individual Contribution/Local Leadership		Freedom: Entrepreneurial/Freedom to Structure
Interdependent/Self-Governing	Solve Their Own Problems/Empowerment/ Encouragement	Humane-Oriented/ Relational	Relational: Empowerment/Encouragement/ Relationship-Focused
Mutual Vision		Charismatic /Value-Based/ Spiritually Empowered	Charisma: Charismatic/Value-Based/ Spiritual

Charisma

The first theme, or leadership trait, that emerged is *charisma*.[5] The GLOBE study identified this important trait, noting it as being crucial for effective global leadership.[6] Charisma includes having a strong spiritual foundation and a strong set of core values when viewed from the broader study on mission leadership. Kirk Franklin speaks to the importance of the *Missio Dei,* highlighting the work of the Trinity. He strengthens it in his missional leadership model by advocating spiritual practices as key to leadership within

---

[5] Yeh, 2016, 38. (Here, Yeh highlights the inspirational aspects of the Medici family as an example of this thematic element).
[6] House, Robert et al., 2014., xv., 58, 260, 268.

the Wycliffe Global Alliance.[7] This is also picked up in the Lausanne[8] and historical literature by Doug Birdsall.[9] Moreover, it shows up in the studies on mission structures and movements.[10]

Charisma, as a theme, is seen in the literature as more than just having charismatic traits or personality. It involves strength of character, trustworthiness, and a faithful presence. It involves holding and maintaining a set of core values. At the same time, there are occasions where charismatic catalysts become pivotal for movements, especially in the more entrepreneurial efforts. It is intriguing to consider the significance of inspiration or charisma from God himself, particularly in the lives of mission leaders throughout history. God is the key sustainer of the leader as well as the movement, reflecting the truth of John 15 that those who remain in the "true vine" – Jesus – will bear much fruit. God inspires us, his followers, through his character and spiritual sustenance in such a manner that, as we remain connected to him, we lead well.

Collaboration

Collaboration is another central theme that is supported throughout the literature on polycentrism. Whether it is the theological collaboration of the *perichoresis* of the Trinity,[11] or collective and collaborative practices from both the governance models[12] or church and mission structures,[13] working together in a shared participative manner is necessary for effective global leadership. J.R. Woodward draws from Ephesians 4 to emphasize the importance of collaboration. This is also noted in the network and collaborative forms of leadership reviewed about movement leadership.[14] For example, Theodore Esler showed the importance of bricolage, or cooperative, organizations working together, and Jehu Hanciles spoke of movements needing a "multiplicity" of leaders rather than one single leader. Even the GLOBE study noted the importance of "participatory leadership" for effective

---

[7] Franklin, Crough, and Crough, 2017, 597, 612.
[8] Birdsall, Doug. 'Conflict and Collaboration: A Narrative History and Analysis of the Interface between the Lausanne Committee for World Evangelization and the World Evangelical Fellowship, the International Fellowship of Evangelical Mission Theologians, and the AD 2000 Movement.' Ph.D. thesis, Middlesex University, 2013, 257.
[9] Birdsall, 2013, 217.
[10] Morse, 1998, 229-238. Also, Franklin, Crough, and Crough, 2017, 235.
[11] McGrath, Alister. *Christian Theology: An Introduction*, 3rd ed. Oxford: Blackwell, 2011, 325.
[12] Ostrom, 2009, 411; Brohm. 2005, 42, 173.
[13] Franklin, Crough, and Crough, 2017, 235.
[14] Bainbridge, 1997, 3. Also see Addison, 2015; Zald and Ash. 1966, 327-341; Schneider, et al. 2003, 152.

global leadership.[15] The literature from mission history captures this as well.[16] Augmenting these findings included the literature on missiology, solidifying it as a key thematic element of polycentric leadership.[17] For mission movements, collaboration is central to a Polycentric Mission Leadership model. It is in the synergy of working together in partnership that collective wisdom is discovered, and effective mission becomes more feasible.

Communal

The third theme for Polycentric Mission Leadership is a *communal* approach to leadership. The Trinity is the embodiment of a community between the Father, Son, and Holy Spirit.[18] The literature on polycentric structures values interconnected communities and leadership in community as highlighted by Franklin's research on the Wycliffe Global Alliance.[19] It is also seen in the contractual and cooperative undertakings in the governance models.[20] These are augmented by the findings about team leadership in the GLOBE study as well.[21] Movement Theory, networks, and collaborative leadership models also embody these important traits.[22] Finally, it shows itself in the missiology and Lausanne literature as well.[23] Leading through community is clearly an integral part of a Polycentric Mission Leadership model. In the fellowship and family-like atmosphere of serving together, leaders gain perspective and insights from one another and function more effectively through checks and balances, holding each other to higher standards and modeling the collective behaviors they esteem and seek to engender toward fulfilling their mutual vision and mission.

Entrepreneurism

Entrepreneurism is another important theme for Polycentric Mission Leadership.[24] The governance and network material make this abundantly clear. Those studies reveal how crucial self-governance and freedom are for

---

[15] House, et al. 2014, 55 and 65-66.
[16] Oladipo, Caleb O. 'How Indigenous Traders brought Christianity to Northern Nigeria.' In Essamuah, Casely B. and David Ngaruiya, eds. *Communities of Faith in Africa and the African Diaspora: In Honor of Dr. Tite Tienou with Additional Essays on World Christianity*. Eugene, OR: Wipf & Stock, 2013, 180-195.
[17] *The Common Call*, Scotland Assembly Hall, Edinburgh. June 6, 2010.Edinburgh Listening Group Report, 10. See also, Lederleitner, 2016.
[18] Newbigin, 1995, 29, 65.
[19] Morse, 1998, 229-238.
[20] Scholte, 2004, 3.
[21] House, et al. 2014, xv., 58, 260, 268.
[22] Hesselgrave, et al. 1978: 318; Logan, King, and Fischer-Wright. 2008, 7.
[23] Schreiter, Robert. 2011, 92. and Dahle, Dahle and Jorgensen, 2014, 20-21. See the Lausanne connection as well: Birdsall, 2013, 295-296.
[24] Yeh, 2016, 38.

local teams to operate independently in order to be most effective.[25] It is liberating and inspiring when leaders have entrepreneurial freedom, as that engenders more effective leadership. This is especially true in relation to mission movements that thrive in a culture of risk-taking, entrepreneurship, experimentation, and innovation.[26] This came out in both the Lausanne studies and surprisingly even in the mission structures research.[27]

For the GLOBE study, this particular theme relates to an aspect of effective leadership that was only found in certain areas, however. The correlation to freedom is the trait they label as *autonomous*. This trait has noted success measures, but mostly in individualist societies and less so in collective ones. Thus, while the GLOBE study considers it to be one of their top traits for effective global leadership, they also noted that it was with mixed results.[28]

Relational

A *relational* dimension is also present in the literature. The GLOBE study labeled this trait *humane-oriented*, defining it as a leader's ability to empower others.[29] Likewise, the governance material acknowledged that polycentric leaders galvanized local communities to solve their own problems while providing encouragement along the way.[30] As for church and missions' structures, encouragement of interdependent teams happens within the community.[31]

Similar to the theme of charisma, the relational theme was not present in the historical literature for this study. It could be that history is not a subject that lends itself to highlighting more relational aspects of leadership, or simply that further research needs to be conducted. However, this theme is prevalent in the remaining research, including the Lausanne material, which has a dimension of history within it.[32]

Diversity

Finally, the sixth theme is *diversity*. Leaders who value and recognize diversity are able to work within regions, networks, and governance models,

---

[25] Aligica, 2012, 2.

[26] Logan, 2008, 14.

[27] Walker, Simon. *The Undefended Leader Trilogy*. Oxford: Human Ecology Partners, 2011, 359. See for structures: Cattan, Nadine. 2007, 65-74.

[28] House, 2013, 55. House et. al. use the term "autonomous" which can be somewhat aligned with the theme of Freedom. It's not as central to the core findings from the study and contradicts the value of communal and collaboration; nevertheless, it is a trait that emerges.

[29] House, 2013, 76.

[30] Aligica, 2012, 2.

[31] Franklin, Crough, and Crough, 2017, 597, 612.

[32] Birdsall, 2013, 219.

leading across cultures, as the GLOBE study reported.[33] The diversity of leadership gifts described in Ephesians 4 also adds credibility to the importance of this trait. This theme is evident in all disciplines, reflecting the importance of diversity to global leadership and polycentric leadership.[34] Diversity does not refer only to leading across regions and nationalities, but also relates to gender, age, social stratification, and sectors.[35] The governance literature viewed the multipolar and regional aspects of this theme as imperative to effective governance.[36] Allen Yeh considers this as crucial to the future of effective mission as well.[37] Thus, for diversity to be fully realized within a Polycentric Mission Leadership model, it must reflect every facet of diversity represented within a network, movement, or society.

Evaluation

Strengths

While Polycentric Mission Leadership[38] is considered an emerging paradigm for leadership, there is as yet insufficient research data (both qualitative and quantitative) to fully evaluate its effectiveness. However, my research reveals that a polycentric leadership approach has promise and deserves further attention.

One of the keys to polycentric leadership is that it draws from the wisdom across cultures, regions, and diverse perspectives. Listening to and valuing diverse voices empowers local leadership across networks, movements, or organizations. It also fosters stronger bonds for teams or employees. As they work together, their relationships are enriched, and this serves to strengthen their shared processes and goals. In addition, it fosters an environment where each locality makes their own decisions based on local contextual circumstances. Amplifying these findings, the interviews among Lausanne Movement leaders reveal more evidence suggesting the relevance of factors

---

[33] House, 2014, 52, 55.

[34] Hollenweger, Walter. 'From Azusa to the Toronto Phenomenon: Historical Roots of the Pentecostal Movement.' In Jürgen Moltmann, and Karl-Josef Kuschel, eds. *Pentecostal Movements as Ecumenical Challenge.* London: SCM, 1996: 3-7 (for history), Birdsall, 2013. 219 (for Lausanne). Morse, 1998, 234 (for Structures).

[35] Jones, Hesterly and Borgatti, 1997, 911-945. Also, Schein, 1985, 143-144) and Esler, 2012, 220. See also, Kennedy, John. "The Most Diverse Gathering Ever," *Christianity Today*, September 2010.

[36] Ostrom, 2009, 411; Scholte, 2004, 3.

[37] Yeh, 2016, back cover quote by IVP editors, 59.

[38] Just as in the Northouse studies, the various models will be noted in this dissertation using capital letters to help understanding them in contrast to one another. Polycentric Leadership is not yet a model reviewed in the Northouse book but as this dissertation reveals, it has enough emerging material to someday be considered as a new theoretical model.

like age, gender, and national perspectives. Seeing the various issue networks operate both independently and interdependently within the overall Lausanne Movement displays these strengths all the more.

The themes that emerge in this model also exist in other leadership theories. For instance, the charisma and relational themes align well with the strengths identified in **Transformational Leadership** [39] theories. Transformational leaders inspire and include followers, moving beyond transactional approaches to leadership. James MacGregor Burns was one of the first to develop this as an approach, highlighting the differences between many leadership approaches that were more transactional in nature versus more relational and transformational in order to inspire followers toward achieving specific outcomes.[40] Building on the model, Bernard Bass reviewed Transformational Leadership through the lens of the followers and how they are inspired, encouraged, and strengthened through a transformational approach.[41] The result: the followers were both transformed and achieved transformative results in their industries. The relational dimensions in Transformational Leadership are present in the relational dimensions of polycentric leadership as well.

Northouse includes **Charismatic Leadership** within this transformational approach, showing the similarities present in the two models.[42] Charismatic leadership is a theoretical model that has been researched over decades.[43] Robert House espoused Charismatic Leadership Theory, which highlights the inspirational qualities of leaders who inspire others through their own confidence, dominance, and strong moral values.[44] Followers, in turn, are inspired by the high demands placed on them by leaders and the shared moral aspirations with those leaders. This is similar to Polycentric Mission Leaders who gain insight and perspective through their reliance on God, which then enables them to influence and inspire those they lead and with whom they collaborate.

---

[39] Downton, J. V. (1973). *Rebel leadership: Commitment and Charisma in a Revolutionary Process.* New York: Free Press. And most importantly, Burns, James MacGregor. *Leadership.* New York: Harper Collins, 1978, 25. As well as Bass, Bernard M. *Leadership and Performance beyond Expectations.* New York: Free Press, 19–31.

[40] Burns, 1978, 18ff.

[41] Bass, 1985, 20ff.

[42] Northouse, 2013, 187. For Charismatic Leadership, see House, Robert A. 1976 *Theory of Charismatic Leadership.* Working Paper Series 76-06. University of Toronto, October 1976.

[43] Bennis and Nanus, 1985. Kouzes and Posner, 1995.

[44] House, 1985. See also the work of Conger, J. A., and Kanungo, R. N. *Charismatic Leadership in Organizations.* Thousand Oaks, CA: Sage, 1998.

Polycentric leadership also shares commonalities with Authentic Leadership in the development of the trustworthiness of leaders.[45] **Authentic Leadership** emerged in response to many of the ethical crises occurring in the world, according to Northouse, and is one of the newer approaches in the spectrum of leadership study. Authentic Leadership is similar to Transformational Leadership in its relational focus and the interaction between the leader and follower. Bruce Avolio, Fred Walumbwa, and Todd Weber describe it as leadership with self-awareness, transparency, a balanced perspective, and a strong moral compass.[46] This correlates well with the charisma theme in polycentric leadership. Given that charisma is more than just a charismatic presence or inspirational influence, its core strength comes from a depth of character and moral trustworthiness.

Servant Leadership Theory shares the relational, communal, and collaborative traits of polycentric leadership. These are leaders who care for others and draw out the strength of others rather than focusing primarily on vision and direction.[47] Robert Greenleaf was an advocate for servant leadership, focusing more on the behaviors of leaders through their service to their followers and organizations. In this approach, leaders put the followers first by empowering their initiative and helping them develop their full potential.[48] Greenleaf states:

> [Servant leadership] begins with the natural feeling that one wants to serve, to serve *first*. Then conscious choice brings one to aspire to lead … The difference manifests itself in the care taken by the servant – first to make sure that other people's highest priority needs are being served. The best test … is: do those served grow as persons; do they, *while being served,* become healthier, wiser, freer, more autonomous, more likely themselves to become servants? *And,* what is the effect on the least privileged in society; will they benefit, or, at least, will they not be further deprived?[49]

Larry Spears built on the concept, defining a set of common characteristics.[50] These ten dimensions include: listening, empathy, healing,

---

[45] Shamir, B., and Eilam, G. 'Authentic leadership measurement and development: Challenges and Suggestions.' In Gardner, W. L., B. J. Avolio, and F. O. Walumbwa (eds.), *Authentic Leadership Theory and Practice: Origins, effects, and development.* Oxford: Elsevier Science, 2005, 227-251; Northouse, 2013, 253.

[46] Avolio, 2009, 421-449.

[47] Northouse, 2013.

[47] Northouse, 2013, 231.

[48] Greenleaf, R. K. *The servant as leader.* Westfield, IN: Greenleaf Center for Servant Leadership, 1970, 15ff.

[49] Greenleaf, R. K. 1970, 15.

[50] Spears, L. C. "Tracing the Past, Present, and Future of Servant-Leadership." In L. C. Spears and M. Lawrence (eds.), *Focus on leadership: Servant-leadership for the 21st century.* New York: John Wiley, 2002, 1–16.

awareness, persuasion, conceptualization, foresight, stewardship, commitment to people growth, and community building. From these frameworks, others have formed a model.[51] These aspects of leadership overlap with polycentric leadership themes in displaying traits that are vital for a relational, communal approach to leading well. From this approach, collaborative leadership is fostered.

The relational, communal, and collaborative themes of polycentric leadership align with the attributes identified in **Team Leadership Theory**.[52] In *Leadership: Theory and Practice,* Susan E. Kogler Hill notes the development of this idea from the efficiency models from the Japanese industry.[53] Today, these are known as *kaizen* models, where continuous improvement is the standard. Toyota has made this particularly effective, advocating for what they call "The Toyota Way".[54] Carl Larson and Frank LaFasto highlight these important collaborative factors in Team Leadership.[55] Perhaps more than others looking at this model, the two note the importance of relational and communal elements. The Team Leadership model includes a complex set of behaviors; nevertheless, it highlights important features of leading well. This approach connects with the collaborative theme from polycentric leadership in this study.

The freedom theme is present in both **Contingency Theory**[56] and **Situational Theory**.[57] Fred Fiedler developed Contingency Theory to highlight how a leader's particular style might fit a particular context.[58]

---

[51] See the questionnaire developed by Liden and Wayne: Liden, R. C., Wayne, S. J., Zhao, H., and Henderson, D. "Servant Leadership: Development of a Multidimensional Measure and Multi-Level Assessment." *Leadership Quarterly,* 19, 2008, 161–177.

[52] Levi, D. *Group Dynamics for Teams.* Thousand Oaks, CA: Sage, 2011. See also: Mankin, D., Cohen, S. G., and Bikson, T. K. *Teams and Technology.* Boston, MA: Harvard Business School Press,1996; Kogler Hill, Susan. 2015. 'Team Leadership Model.' In Northouse, Peter *Leadership: Theory and Practice.* Thousand Oaks, CA: Sage, 287-318.

[53] Kogler Hill, 2015, 288. See also Zaccaro, S. J., Heinen, B., and Shuffler, M. 'Team leadership and team effectiveness.' In E. Salas, G. F. Goodwin, and C. S. Burke (eds.), *Team Effectiveness in Complex Organizations: Cross–disciplinary Perspectives and Approaches.* New York: Taylor & Francis, 2009, 83-111.

[54] Sakai Y., Sugano T., "Maeda T.-Introduction of Toyota Production System to promote innovative manufacturing," *Fujitsu Science Technology Japan,* 43, January, 2007, 14-22.

[55] Larson, C. E., and LaFasto, F. M. J. *Teamwork: What must go right/what can go wrong.* Newbury Park, CA: Sage, 1989.

[56] Fiedler, F. E. (1964). "A contingency model of leadership effectiveness." In L. Berkowitz (ed.), *Advances in Experimental Social Psychology.* Vol. 1, 149-190.

[57] Hersey, P., and Blanchard, K. H. (1969a). "Life-Cycle Theory of Leadership." *Training and Development Journal,* 23, 26-34. See also Northouse, 2013 (situational), 99, (contingency) 183.

[58] Fiedler, 1964, 149-190.

Similarly, Paul Hersey and Ken Blanchard developed Situational Theory to highlight the different approaches needed in various settings.[59] Contingency Theory is focused more on the leader, while Situational Theory is based more on the needs of the particular context. In both cases, flexibility based on the person or situation is imperative. This is where the freedom theme from polycentric leadership is relevant. These theories value the freedom of the leader to structure and develop the network or movement as necessary.

Like the other theories highlighted, polycentric leadership shares the diverse theme with Northouse's findings on **culture and leadership**.[60] This also aligns with the GLOBE study research. Nancy Adler and Susan Bartholomew were among the first to outline the importance of these cultural nuances,[61] and the most widely researched work in this arena are the ongoing studies by Geert Hofstede,[62] who noted five dimensions of cultural leadership: power distance, uncertainty avoidance, individualism–collectivism, masculinity–femininity, and long-term–short-term orientation. Both the GLOBE study and Hofstede's findings show how vital diversity is across a number of categories for global leadership. The six themes discovered in this research project complement these other leadership theories, amplifying how important this theme is for Polycentric Mission Leadership.

Criticisms

Because the idea of polycentric leadership is new, there is not enough empirical evidence to test it as a theory. That said, just as critiques are being offered for other emergent ideas, this new approach is being reviewed and tested. Similar to the critique of the GLOBE study, some could argue that the themes for polycentric leadership are vague and ill-defined.[63] It is also important to consider differences between the GLOBE study and Hofstede's research.[64] The GLOBE study relied heavily on Implicit Leadership Theory, which frames leadership based on people's perceptions.[65] This approach, while

---

[59] Hersey, P., and Blanchard, K. H. "Management of Organizational Behavior: Utilizing Human Resources." *Academy of Management Journal*, 12 (4), 1969, 526.
[60] Northouse, 2013, 396ff.
[61] Adler, N. J., and Bartholomew, S. "Managing Globally Competent People." *Academy of Management Executive*, 6,1992, 52-65.
[62] Hofstede, G. *Culture's consequences: International differences in work-related values*. Beverly Hills, CA: Sage, 1980; Hofstede, G. *Culture's Consequences: Comparing Values, Behaviors, Institutions, and Organizations Across Nations*. Thousand Oaks, CA: Sage, 2001.
[63] Northouse, 2013, 406.
[64] See Hofstede's critiques here: Hofstede, G. "What Did GLOBE really Measure? Researchers' Minds versus Respondents' Minds." *Journal of International Business Studies*, 37, 6, 2006, 882-896; Hofstede, G. "The GLOBE debate: Back to relevance." *Journal of International Business Studies*, vol. 41, 2010, 1339–1346.
[65] Lord, R., and Maher, K. J. *Leadership and Information Processing: Linking Perceptions and Performance*. Boston, MA: Unwin Hyman, 1991.

promising, examines leaders' perception of their effectiveness rather than their behaviors. And most of the research in leadership studies has focused on behavior rather than perception. Also similar to both the GLOBE study and Trait Theory (a leadership theory focused on attributes of leadership), it may be difficult to isolate the six themes that have emerged compared to various situational or contextual environments.[66] This challenge is analyzed by Gary Evans in his overview of culture research and corporate boards, where he mentions the disagreements between Hofstede and the GLOBE study and notes the challenges inherent in culture studies. While Evans affirms the essential findings of these studies, he suggests further research to supplement the results and bring further clarity.[67]

While the next section of this chapter will review a few emerging models of polycentric leadership, further research on these themes would elicit a stronger behavior set for global leaders. This could resolve the vagueness of the emerging themes and lend credibility to polycentric leadership as a potential theory. It would also be helpful to develop a research tool similar to what was designed by the GLOBE study that could measure these six common themes quantitatively. The narrative findings from the Lausanne interviews provide substantive data affirming these six themes, but it would be helpful if a tool could be devised to refine the behaviors from these six themes for a polycentric leadership model.

Finally, it would be worthwhile to review other emerging polycentric leadership models which could address these criticisms. To begin that process, several models are reviewed using the Northouse approach in the next section to bolster the findings.[68] Then, I will share my analysis of the Lausanne Movement, which provides a strong data set for an emerging theoretical model.

Application: Examples of Polycentric Leadership

In this section, I review emergent models from different contexts to further evaluate the developing theory. These contexts include the local church, a larger mission organization, and a leader development ministry. One of the

---

[66] Northouse, 2013, 406.

[67] Evans, Gary Llewellyn. "Culture Research and Corporate Boards." *American International Journal of Contemporary Research*. 3:5, 2013. See also, Franke, G.R. and Richey, R.G. "Improving generalizations from multi-country comparisons in international business research." *Journal of International Business Studies*, Vol. 41, 2010,1275–1293; Tung, R.L. and Verbeke, A. "Beyond Hofstede and GLOBE: Improving the quality of cross-cultural research." *Journal of International Business Studies*, Vol. 41, 2010, 1259–1274.

[68] As noted above, the Northouse approach to evaluating leadership theories and models is recognized as the standard thus it is used here as an evaluative framework in the next section looking at models.

examples within the larger organization is also highlighted as a stand-alone model from South America. Each serves as an example of the model in action and provides the opportunity for evaluation of this emerging theory.

Missional Church Model

J.R. Woodward presents a polycentric model in his book *Creating a Missional Culture*. He builds the model on an equipping paradigm based on Ephesians 4. His model identifies the apostle, prophet, evangelist, prophet, and teacher, which he describes as a storyteller, as equippers of the church who function based on their giftedness.[69] Woodward describes this model as a shift from a hierarchical model to a polycentric approach, where the equippers empower others to foster the mission of the church.[70] He refers to Roland Allen's view of Paul's approach to ministry to undergird his theological approach.[71] This model is not dependent only on the equippers, but also on the central work of the Holy Spirit,[72] and Woodward highlights how the Spirit is the agent behind the equipper leaders in the missional congregations.

In laying out the model, Woodward shares how the equipping team leads like geese in flight, who share the leadership load and take turns based on their giftings. In describing the relational dimension of the team, he offers the Trinity as a model, which "is interdependent, communal, relational, participatory, self-surrendering and self-giving. This is how the equippers should lead. In addition, it is important for the equippers to have mutual respect for one another, appreciating the gifting and experience of each person, giving weight to each."[73] He then suggests using this communal approach to decision-making, which relies on the group rather than an individual point of view. This creates a participatory element of leadership and a decentralized approach that informs how the church leaders capture vision, which should actually come from the Spirit's leading rather than their own initiative.[74]

Woodward refers to the functioning of a Quaker congregation to describe how his model works. In their case, the leaders gather for worship, noting that leadership, meetings, and decision-making are, in essence, part of their communal worship. In this particular congregation, 12 leaders gather, building community, worshipping together, and spending time in silence before discussing issues related to the work of the church. Remarkably, all issues are decided with unanimous support. Although running a church this way can be

---

[69] Woodward, 2013, 58.
[70] Woodward, 2013, 60.
[71] Woodward citing the work of Roland Allen, *Mission Activities Considered in Relation to the Manifestation of the Spirit*. London: World Dominion, Press, 1927, 30.
[72] Woodward, 2013, 212-213.
[73] Woodward, 2013, 214.
[74] Woodward, 2013, 215.

inefficient, ownership is high due to the participatory nature of having all key people involved in leadership, which is a strength.[75]

This example, however, only reflects aspects of polycentrism as a theoretical leadership model. By focusing on leadership systems within particular churches, it misses the regional aspects critical to some of the themes existent within the overall leadership theory.

Mission Organization Model

A missional leadership model proposed by Kirk Franklin in reshaping the Wycliffe Global Alliance (WGA) is also multifaceted, drawing from an eclectic array of research, and includes polycentric approaches in its operation. The WGA moved from a centralized leadership ecosystem or institutional organism to a model encompassing leadership across the globe, forming an alliance of 100 organizations sharing a decentralized form of governance. This body operates communally, casting vision, making decisions, and collaborating throughout the Alliance.[76]

This communal approach to WGA's leadership shifts power away from a centralized location to the margins.[77] One of the key features of their model is providing equality of leadership alongside exchanging the lead position for the community as a whole. In other words, leaders come and go within their ecosystem so that they take turns assuming the lead position within their structural system. This is an interconnected, culturally diverse community of leaders and a model that is decentralized with limited central controls and structures.[78]

Leader Development Model

Another model that uses a polycentric approach is the movement I have the privilege of leading. Asian Access still had an official operating structure with a governing board, president, and typical flow chart; however, we have adapted the distribution of our leadership using a polycentric model of leadership to foster collaboration, participation, freedom, and diverse perspectives. We envision ourselves more as a community than an organization, as our vision states: "a vibrant community of servant leaders … leading the church across Asia."[79]

Our core leadership involves a ministry team, an infrastructure team, and a missionary-focused team. All three are made up of both staff and volunteer leaders and seek to represent every region within our overall network. In addition, our advisory systems include a Vision Council, which is represented

---

[75] Woodward, 2013, 216-218.
[76] Franklin, Crough, and Crough, 2017.
[77] Franklin, 2016, 241.
[78] Franklin, 2016, 242.
[79] Asian Access Vision and Mission Statements, 2019.

by leaders from many of the countries we operate in. We make decisions collaboratively through a deeply communal process and each team has the freedom to structure and make decisions based on the values of the movement and our collective vision and mission.

At the ground level, each country makes its own decisions in a similar communal fashion with working teams, which are initially formed in consultation with the Asian Access leadership team. Future vision is achieved through a collaborative and prayerful discernment process. For the past few years, all of these leadership teams, as well as many on-the-ground participants, volunteers, employees, and missionaries, have had the opportunity to speak into the formation of our next multiyear strategic plan. In this way, God speaks through the community and inspires the vision and direction (charisma) from within our midst as we listen to him collectively to discern our future.

As each country develops within our ecosystem, it becomes more and more independent in how it structures, leads, and designs our overall approach. Thus, Asian Access looks substantially different in China than it does in India or Cambodia. We share the same core values and overall vision, but the expression of those in each location can be quite distinct. Even the language used can differ, where some countries do not even use the name "Asian Access" to describe the movement in their nation. In this way, each of these national leadership teams are practicing forms of Polycentric Mission Leadership.

Mission Association Model

Nydia García-Schmidt, America's director for the Wycliffe Global Alliance, has witnessed this emergent polycentric model in the ongoing work of networks of Bible translators working together in Peru. It was 2013 and the Interethnic Evangelical Association of Peru (ACIEP, Asociación Cristiana Interétnica del Perú), a new association of nine organizations, had just begun to work together. Some came in wondering why they were there but, as the communal leadership process continued, García-Schmidt was impressed. She described the outcomes of the meeting as follows:

> As I listened to ACIEP's staff, it was clear that they had a strong ownership for the part they played in making God's Word accessible to their communities. They spoke in great detail about ensuring that their work was actually having the desired impact. I could identify among them both men and women who were problem solvers, visionaries, leaders, paradigm shifters, strategic thinkers and community builders. When presenting some WGA principles about community, and Biblical foundations for the work of Bible translation, I began to sense a revitalized outlook among them. All these signs demonstrate aspects of community empowerment ... The members of ACIEP were happy to know that they had a space and a voice, not just in their local situation, but also in the global scenario. Near the end of our time together, I asked the ACIEP leadership and all

who were participating in the meeting to consider what they could contribute to the larger Bible translation movement – a question they had not been asked before. Then they debated among themselves how to include more organizations and people in their association – mainly because they found value in creating capacity for others.

ACIEP is one of many emerging polycentric centres of influence realizing the important role they play in developing sustainable and contextualized approaches to taking God's word to their own indigenous communities. In addition, they increasingly understand how their voices and experiences are vital for the larger mission movement. By embracing the values of affirming and nurturing polycentric communities, a participatory approach is fostered between global and local, recognizing that community empowerment is acting upon this vital inter-linkage – regardless of the nature of the ministry focus.[80]

García-Schmidt clearly sees the value of the polycentric leadership model as she assesses the ACIEP.

The above models provide a background for reviewing the potential of an emerging theory of Polycentric Mission Leadership. They formulate aspects of what is found in the literature related to polycentrism and set a foundation for looking at the Lausanne Movement.

Summary

In essence, a polycentric model of leadership has the potential to form an approach to leadership that is multicentered and shared. It is leadership that forms in community, drawing from the diversity of the movement to provide wisdom, guidance, and direction. It gives freedom to each location (region, function, location, etc.) to operate based on the common, collective commitments determined by the community and shaped by the charismatic presence of the Trinitarian Lord, foundational to orthodox Christian faith. It is a model that has historical precedent and continues to grow. It shares many strengths with other leadership models and theories and holds promise for future mission leadership.

I conclude this chapter by describing the methodology to test this idea within the context of the Lausanne Movement.

Conclusion

These six themes – charismatic, collaborative, communal, relational, entrepreneurial, and diverse – add further depth to the work that Woodward and Franklin have already accomplished on polycentric leadership. The various models reviewed in these chapters, when synthesized, form a stronger

---

[80] García-Schmidt, Nydia. "Community Empowerment." In Franklin, Crough, and Crough, 2017, 43ff.

core model for Polycentric Mission Leadership. Even though these six attributes are important for the polycentric leadership model, they are not present across all spectrums of the literature reviews.

There were two themes in particular which were not well represented from my study of the literature. The relational theme was not represented in the historical studies and the charisma theme was absent from the governance literature. (This latter may have been due to the fact that the focus of this research was on operations of governance rather than the specific traits behind the governing models.)

Even though the GLOBE study didn't comment on the freedom theme, it did identify a related trait – autonomous. The challenge is that this particular trait was isolated to more individualist societies rather than collective cultures.[81] It was a trait that was positive in some cases and negative in others.

The Polycentric Mission Leadership model recognizes multiple spheres of influence which can include, but are not limited to, geography, ethnicity, regions, and nationalities. In addition, diversity is a clear indicator within the literature overall. Thus, identity elements of age and gender also play an important role.

Ideally, this is a type of leadership that is inclusive of the varied centers of influence within one's network or movement, or, as in the case of Wycliffe, that draws from the rich tapestry of wisdom across these platforms and sectors to guide the movement in mission. From each of these diverse peoples and platforms, a community is formed that is rooted in Christ. Inspired by the Holy Spirit, this community operates in a collective fashion to empower and release the gifts and potential of each person. This inspiration is where vision (part of the charisma theme) comes from. As God works in our midst, we gain strength, develop character and core values, and gain vision for the mission, the *Missio Dei*. Each community forms an interdependent team working together through shared perspectives and collective yet multilayered processes. In essence, they are an entrepreneurial network, catalyzing self-governing entities, set on fulfilling the mission to which they have been called. Each grouping has the authority to lead as the local situation requires them to lead, and they function in unity, but with diversity of expression, leadership, and governance.

The Trinity is their model as the Father, Son, and Holy Spirit operate together as one but also through their differing roles and expressions. As such, they model interdependence as three distinct expressions working as one. Stanley Grenz captures this well: "The three members of the Trinity are 'person' precisely because they are persons-in-relationship; that is, their personal identities emerge out of their reciprocal relations." Further, he explains that "[t]he attendant ontology of personhood suggests that the Creator's intent that humans be the representation of the divine reality means that the goal of human existence is to be persons-in-relation after the pattern

---

[81] House, 2014, 79-80.

of the perichoretic life disclosed in Jesus Christ." [82] In sharing about polycentric mission, Patrick Fung highlights this as well: "A biblical cooperation involves serving together as a community in unity but not uniformity. Giving space to one another, *kenosis*, involves emptying self, letting go of our own space, preferences and agenda."[83]

The following chapter applies this research methodology to leaders within the Lausanne Movement.

---

[82] Grenz, Stanley J. *The Social God and the Relational Self: A Trinitarian Theology of the Imago Dei* Louisville, KY: Westminster John Knox, 2001, 332.

[83] Fung, Patrick. "Cooperation in a Polycentric World." A presentation at WEA MC Global Consultation, Panama 2016, 2. Fung draws from others as well. See Woods, Paul, "Perichoresis and Koinonia: Implications of our Fellowship with God for the Changing Missionary Endeavor." *Mission Round Table*, 10, 1, January, 2015 and Moltmann, Jürgen, *Trinity in the Kingdom of God*. London: SCM: 2000.

5. Interviews within the Lausanne Movement

Introduction

Interviews of leaders with global mission experience bolster the theoretical underpinnings of a move towards Polycentric Mission Leadership. In conversation with a handful of scholars and practitioners, I chose the Lausanne Movement as a global network to further test the idea. The history of the movement in mission and its global landscape provided an ideal ecosystem to review the emergent model. I chose 33 leaders from across the world who, according to leaders within and outside the movement, have a particularly successful reach and influence. They are either in significant posts within the movement overall or their issue-based networks have substantive traction that have produced pivotal documents within their sector or sphere for the future of mission overall.

The findings from these interviews highlight the six themes (or what some might call traits) discerned from the Polycentric Mission Leadership model detailed in the previous chapter. Below I share common themes and the corresponding interview data, along with select key quotations from some of the interviewees.

Common Themes

Collaborative

From my review of the literature, the concept of collaboration stands out as a key feature for leading in a polycentric manner. There is power in participating in a network, a collective, or in a shared fashion, and for the Lausanne Movement, these networks lend themselves to achieving common goals even across the diversity of regions and cultural perspectives.

A number of strands from the chapter on polycentric structures fit under this collaborative theme. [1] These include: leadership that functions in collaboration and through a network and leadership in community – especially in interconnected communities. For polycentric governance, the importance of shared participation and collective practice relate to the collaborative cross-over theme.[2] In addition, the idea of contractual or cooperative leadership comes under this rubric. In the case of polycentric governance, collectives

---

[1] See Table "Chart of Crossover Themes", 62.
[2] See Table "Chart of Crossover Themes", 62.

across differing sectors sometimes form contracts to solidify their common objectives. At other times, they simply work as a cooperative to benefit one another even if their goals may differ. The GLOBE study reinforces the importance of participative leadership and team-orientation.

Of the 33 people interviewed, 24 responded in ways confirming this collaborative stream of thinking. They emphasized the importance of working together as either key to their recruitment within the movement or network they lead, the key to their success within the network they serve or the movement overall, or to advising others desiring to serve within the Lausanne ecosystem. Overall, this theme was the second most mentioned in the interviews.

Nana Yaw Offei Awuku, global associate director for generations,[3] in answering the question about missiological omissions, captured this theme well: "Nobody anywhere should set the agenda for the Global Church today. It must be a collaborative effort. All of us must do it together. No one can do it alone."[4] Similarly, Anne-Christine Bataillard, former catalyst for children and evangelism, when sharing about crucial missiological values, noted:

> [To be effective] we need to stop looking at our differences, respect each other and work together. We will then have much more impact ... [We need] to collaborate or partner among churches more and between organizations and churches, with the attitude of serving each other and the view of empowering the other. And, not impose our views or methods or take advantage.[5]

All of the leaders I interviewed highlighted the crucial importance of collaboration for leading in mission today. That said, the work of collaboration is easier said than done. Phill Butler, catalyst for partnership, said, "Everybody talks about collaboration, but nobody does it. It's an idealized and realized value – there's a huge difference."[6] As a catalyst for partnership, Butler was frustrated by the few examples of collaboration in mission. However, today there appears to be more collaboration developing within mission circles than in my several decades of mission leadership. Butler mentioned that even *Harvard Business Review*[7] had an article suggesting that the new C-Suite office should include a chief collaboration officer because of how important the issue is. He suggests that the Lausanne Movement has enormous potential

---

[3] Titles for the Lausanne Leaders focus on their current roles. Given that this study was conducted over a few years, some of those titles have changed. For instance: many of the titles formerly were senior associates but today are labeled as catalysts.
[4] Awuku, Nana Yaw Offei. Interview via Skype, 2018.
[5] Bataillard, Anne-Christine. Interview, 2019.
[6] Butler, Phill. Interview, 2014.
[7] Hansen, Morton and Tapp, Scott "Who should be your Chief Collaboration Officer?" *Harvard Business Review*, October 11, 2010.

but "has the single most challenging collaborative initiative."[8] The reason, Butler says, is because "the higher you go in abstraction, the higher the difficulty of keeping people's attention and collaboration."[9] Ruslan Maliuta of the children at risk network, agreed: "Everyone talks about collaboration but very few people get to the point where they really experience this and partner."[10] That said, both Butler and Maliuta were strong advocates of collaboration, recognizing its value in being fruitful in mission leadership.

Today, collaboration and partnership are making great strides and seeing fruitful progress. Michael Oh, CEO of the Movement, said it this way: "Perhaps the greatest opportunity is ground level, and broader level, collaboration."[11] Later, he added, "The vision for Lausanne IV, in fact, is to mobilize the Global Church toward catalytic collaboration to address the greatest opportunities and gaps of the Great Commission."[12] Doug Birdsall, the former executive chair, noted "a trend toward collaboration and community."[13] This idea will come up again as we talk about charisma.

Two leaders noted how important this theme is for success in the Lausanne Movement when sharing how leadership is different today than it was 10 or 15 years ago. Lindsay Olesberg, former catalyst for scripture engagement, states that, to serve as a leader today, "there's an expectation of higher levels of collaboration and partnership within your own organization and teams."[14] Bodil Skjøtt, catalyst for Jewish evangelism, expressed it this way: "We can do more together than if we stay by ourselves ... [Now] people are more willing to network. Lausanne has introduced me to a strong emphasis on partnership and networking."[15] Highlighting this further, Birdsall shares, "You have to realize that Lausanne is set up to bring out the best in one another by connecting them and providing resources to strengthen them. It doesn't compete with other organizations. It's a movement, not an institution. Generous in its spirit. It's strategic in convening leaders at appropriate intervals."[16]

These leaders confirm the idea found in the literature on polycentrism that collaboration is a key theme for polycentric leadership. In order for a leader to be effective within the Lausanne Movement today, that person must be collaborative in their approach, willing to work in a team-centered paradigm where no one rises above the others, but works together toward the goals of their particular network within the movement.

---

[8] Butler, 2014.
[9] Butler, 2014.
[10] Maliuta, Ruslan. Interview, 2018.
[11] Oh, Michael. Interview, 2015.
[12] Oh, Michael. Correspondence on 28 September 2019.
[13] Birdsall, Doug. Interview, 2015.
[14] Olesberg, Lindsay. Interview, 2018.
[15] Skjøtt, Bodil. Interview, 2018.
[16] Birdsall, 2015.

Communal

The communal theme includes the following key strands: community, contractual or cooperative, own ecosystem, mutual vision, and team. In this theme, cooperation moves to a deeper sense of togetherness. Here, collaborators become a community, establishing a contract where vision is shared so together they can function as a team. In this grouping, ownership is taken to a deeper level of commitment.

In the GLOBE study, two main strands fall under the communal theme: teamwork and participative. Relational and humane elements are included in this as well. When it comes to polycentric governance, the key aspects are shared participation, collective practice, and cooperative undertaking. From the polycentric structure literature, leadership in community takes center stage.

There were 22 leaders among those interviewed who commented on the importance of community and teamwork. When speaking of fruitful kingdom leadership, Samuel Chiang, catalyst for orality, recognized "the ability to bring together people who might create culture together. Trust in the key leader allows others to be comfortable with each other and talk and create. [We need] a new understanding of *koinonia* – a philosophy of *koinonia* at the godhead level means so much."[17] Chiang makes a powerful point in bringing up the biblical concept of *koinonia* and the partnership inherent in the godhead of the Trinity. This offers a rich picture of how leadership can best function today. Leighton Ford, former executive chair, reflected, "[We should] go back to how the Moravians were formed. They all came together and had communion together. It's not a program but life on life mentoring. Leaders come together and listen to the Lord and one another. [It's important to] trust peers and fellow leaders. [It's important] to value others and make sure everybody has a voice."[18]

Olesberg speaks of the power of friendship in relation to this theme as she shares her advice for future Lausanne Movement leaders. She believes that in Lausanne, "good friendships are the coin of the realm. [The] priority of deep relational investment [is important]. People are wondering, 'Are you going to be a part of real community here or not?'"[19] It is apparent that this aspect of polycentric leadership is going to a deeper level of community, to one of forming friendships. Awuku illustrates this further:

> Partnership for global mission will have strength that closely parallels global friendships. I think that in the next years ahead of us, as important as results may

---

[17] Chiang, Samuel. Interview, 2014.
[18] Ford, Leighton. Interview, 2018.
[19] Olesberg, 2018.

be, the strength of authentic relationships of trust, openness, friendship, common shared purpose between global north and south leaders will be critical."[20]

Rob Martin, former catalyst for resource mobilization, expressed that one of Lausanne's strengths was noted by Ray Bakke as the issue networks:

If you look at them, you are capturing the elders of the evangelical church today. We've got the world experts in these networks. Look at the quality of people! Lausanne's strength is in the community that it creates through the meetings and conversation. There is nobody else capable of doing the international conversation that is necessary today.[21]

Building on this communal framework, Patrick Fung, Lausanne board member, put it this way:

Often people talk about vision. It's a given. But the more I'm in the role, the more I feel that you are able to connect with people heart, mind and soul. The connectiveness will build trust that people will follow the leader. That requires vulnerability, openness and ability to connect regularly. I think it's only by sharing lives together, that you can lead. You can lead a meeting, but you need to share lives. A true authentic leadership will be part of the life together – Jesus shared life together. True authentic leadership requires this – that shaped me.

The new generation requires even more vulnerability, more examples of failure than success. More stories of brokenness than achievement and how you recover. Able to listen to their perspective from their generation. Be able to connect to new generation – heart, mind and soul. 30 years ago, you could be a strong leader with a certain kind of hierarchy. Thirty years ago, at OMF, they called the director sir and ma'am. That's not acceptable today. The new generation appreciates openness. Share example of failure and how you overcome. It is much less formal, much more connected … Connected in a different way.[22]

Butler adds further insight when speaking about how leadership has changed over the past 10–15 years: "[Leadership today] is less top-down – hierarchical in style. It's much more in teams and collegial, listening to people, engage people in the process, give them ownership."[23] This certainly is seen in how the issue networks are being developed today. Every issue network is led by a team of at least two or three catalysts coming from different regions of the world, representing differing generations, nationalities, and ethnicities. For the issue network I serve, we have a senior Nigerian social enterprise leader who for years led the International Fellowship of Evangelical Students (IFES)

---

[20] Awuku, 2018.
[21] Martin, Rob. Interview, 2018.
[22] Fung, Patrick. Interview, 2018.
[23] Butler, 2014.

in his region, and a younger Polish woman who serves in the Methodist Church, running her own NGO which serves entities as diverse as the Bible societies, OMF International, and corporate trainers with Chick-fil-A.

Such comments by leaders within the Lausanne Movement point to a clear value of communal leadership. Leaders who work with others in community bring change to their various networks and issue groups and foster an environment that has the momentum to go farther together. As the teams work together, comradery builds, vision coalesces, and action begins to take shape. While this last piece is anecdotal, my sense in working within the Lausanne Movement as a recently appointed network catalyst for leadership development is that there are some very strong communal bonds guiding various elements within the movement overall.[24]

Diverse

Although it does not appear as often as collaborative and communal themes, the third theme – *diverse* – is an important element of polycentric leadership in that it includes having a variety of perspectives in terms of gender, region, age, and cross-cultural acumen.

The strengths of interdependency and self-governing are particularly evident in polycentric structures.[25] Diversity plays an important role as a catalyst for the entrepreneurial element of polycentric structures. This is even more apparent in the literature related to polycentric governance, where diversity of perspective and shared cross-cultural attributes are important. While this theme wasn't addressed directly in the GLOBE study, their research involves operating in diverse ecosystems. It is significant that all three streams of literature addressed diversity, whether directly or indirectly.

The diversity issue was popular among the Lausanne leaders, with 22 of the 33 leaders referring to this topic. Their comments focused on shifting momentum from the West to the Global South or to dynamics related to culture.

Former executive chair Doug Birdsall captures these changes and leadership trends best: "Leadership of Majority World is recognized by global leaders as bringing the freshness and creativity. Leadership has gone from multinational Western initiative to working in many nations."[26] Former board member Esme Bowers also recognized the transition: "The changes of faces since 1997 to today [in leadership]: before it was all white and now it's a big group of black, Asian, and mixed faces. [There is also] a huge swing of women moving into positions of making decisions. Everywhere we go, we need to make a place for women."[27] Former board member Roger Parrott points out

---

[24] This appointment came after the research was complete.
[25] See Table "Chart of Crossover Themes", 62.
[26] Birdsall, 2015.
[27] Bowers, Esme. Interview, 2018.

the differences as well, noting that they struggled in the past: "[We need to] genuinely partner with non-Western leaders in a real partnership. In the past most were marginalized."[28]

Several of those I interviewed saw this change as imperative for global leadership and for the Lausanne Movement. Las Newman, global associate director for regions, captures their beliefs, stating, "[We must] embrace multi-ethnic, multi-cultural church and community in a globalized world. The rise of global Pentecostalism and the growth of Christianity in the Global South [is one the biggest changes I am seeing]." [29] Joseph Vijayam, catalyst for technology, observing the changes in the world, stressed this even more:

> There is a rise of leadership in missions from the Global South. The rise of women in Christian leadership. The rise of younger leaders all over the world that are taking a more significant role. One of the big surprises is that the church in the majority world is both younger and has a higher representation of women than in North America and Europe. We will continue to face this issue of the diaspora and migrant peoples. The priority is to engage people from all over the world. I can't stress the importance of [this enough] … I have a unique vantage point: I live in North America and spend an equal amount of time in India. I get to see with different lenses than most people do. For us (you and I) it's easy to see the differences and recognize the importance of cultural sensitivity to people's priorities. If we don't continue to stress the need to involve people from different parts of the world, we can quickly become irrelevant in places where the church is growing at its most rapid pace.[30]

Some are encouraged by Lausanne's progress on these fronts. Sadiri Joy Tira of the Global Diaspora Network states:

> Global migration and diaspora have accelerated so fast. The world has become borderless. There are cultural borders but because of technology – no longer a global village, but global apartments. The world has shrunk more today than 15 years ago. [For Lausanne], the regional leadership is very diverse. International Deputy Directors[31] are strategically balanced. If you look at a list of Senior Associates – there is a strategic balance of leaders from South, East, West, and North. A broader coalition and infusion of cultural dynamics in the leadership of Lausanne and that reflects the Church leadership. It was not perceived like that in the past. No longer perceived as another Western, imperialistic leadership. In the past, it was another Western-driven, colonial model.[32]

---

[28] Parrott, Roger. Interview, 2018.
[29] Newman, Las. Interview, 2019.
[30] Vijayam, Joseph. Interview, 2018.
[31] Since 2016, this role has been called regional director.
[32] Tira, Sadiri Joy. Interview, 2014.

That's not to say that there isn't room to grow. Samuel Chiang shared a concern: "We have neglected the honor/shame perspective so deeply that we don't know how to regain it. Our theological basis is so shallow that we need to redevelop it … We need a gospel that reaches every place in the world not solely on guilt and innocence."[33]

In summary, Patrick Fung, Lausanne board member, speaks to this theme of diversity well:

> Mission changed from linear to multi-directional, from 'West to the rest' and now to the diaspora, from the diaspora. It is much less linear. We see the emergence of the Global South mission movements. I still think that Lausanne will need to have a bit more input from the majority world and reset their mindset – Western and majority world leaders. The majority of the world needs to come out of the mindset of no power and nothing to contribute (inferiority complex). Not in an arrogant manner. And demonstrate humble godly leadership for the kingdom. Both come together to learn and appreciate one another. Appreciate the gaps. Let's listen to each other.[34]

It is this diversity of leadership that is multigenerational, multinational, multiethnic, multicultural, and diverse in socio-economic and political backgrounds that allows strong bonds to develop. Only these will overcome obstacles, create unified momentum, and catalyze ideas toward a better future.

Entrepreneurial

The fourth theme is *freedom*, which is independence from overarching structures in terms of decision making and setting agendas. This includes the teams' freedom to structure of their own accord, and the more entrepreneurial aspects of leadership that are seen as leadership teams are free to practice their expertise, creatively defining their own realities and managing, collecting, and building their own resources for the areas they oversee. Innovation is necessary for creativity in mission. What I found in my conversations was that, whether it was a conversation about technology, the diversity of the world, communication patterns, or something else, there was a sense that creativity is crucial for leaders. As Zaretsky said, "[We are] constantly looking for innovative ways to engage around spiritual issues and lots of interesting methodologies in our network."[35]

The freedom theme is especially pronounced in the literature on polycentric governance. Several elements from the research on governance highlight how important it is to have entrepreneurial or free operating power. Freedom of the individual and freedom to manage or configure things in their own way were crucial aspects of governing in a polycentric fashion. Developing a group's

---

[33] Chiang, 2014.
[34] Fung, 2018.
[35] Zaretsky, Tuvya. Interview, 2014.

own ecosystem was clearly important in the findings from the governance literature. While this theme wasn't distinct in the GLOBE study, there could be a connection to the spiritual empowerment trait, which necessitates some degree of freedom.

It was interesting that elements of the freedom theme in polycentric governance affirm Kirk Franklin's leadership model. While he posited a new theoretical model for mission leadership that incorporated polycentrism as a feature, in my research a polycentric leadership theoretical model with six key themes stands distinct.

Only 17 of the 33 comments related to the freedom theme. Nevertheless, this theme is well represented in the literature on polycentric governance. Former board chair Ram Gidoomal captures the essence of this theme in his assessment:

> [Mission has changed] from everywhere to everywhere. Decentralization of power from Europe and US to closer to the ground. Shift the power bases to the regions of the mission. [The] secular world is now doing this too. [We should ask] who are the people on the ground and are they being empowered? As Lao Tzu said, "they will all say we did it". The art of letting others have their way. My principle is doing myself out of a job. This operates in a healthy environment.[36]

Emphasizing it to a greater degree, though, is Mac Pier, catalyst for cities, who describes what effective leadership looks like today:

> [We need] starters, incubators, planters ... What makes them effective: risk-takers, Ephesians 3 view of the world. God can do more. Alliance builders. For me, and my role, trying to have a Barnabas style of leadership. Trying to find the Pauls and empower them. Barnabas is a networker and resource provider. Investing in other leaders and other efforts. A dime invested in us is a dollar for others. We try to be multipliers.[37]

Butler amplifies this theme adding:

> Largely because of the radical evolution in communications, power has devolved from the center to the edges. Examples being stockholder revolts. Shareholders can now sit at home and on their computer know the details of the corporation – its health and general performance. Risk-taking is more important today. We need to be risk comfortable. And, we need to adopt the innovation curve. There has to be a dreamer and then the model maker.[38]

---

[36] Gidoomal, Ram. Interview, 2015.
[37] Pier, Mac. Interview, 2019.
[38] Butler, 2014.

Finally, in his assessment of the future of the Lausanne Movement, Tira exhorts, "Lausanne needs to be careful not become an organization run by a CEO. It is a network and movement."[39]

Clearly, polycentric leadership requires freedom of expression and operation. Lausanne leaders recognize something pivotal about polycentric governance: in order to lead well today, there must be the space to guide and shape within one's own group and sphere of influence. Entrepreneurial engines must be activated in order for mission networks to thrive. It is this entrepreneurism that emerges from the Lausanne interviews that captures this theme of freedom. That said, since only about half the interviewees highlighting this sense of entrepreneurialism, more could be done in this regard within the movement. To truly see Polycentric Mission Leadership flourishing within the movement, various regions of the world will be setting their own agendas and leading the way in the life of mission and within the overall movement of Lausanne.

Relational

The fifth theme emerging in this study is *relational* and it includes the elements of empowerment, encouragement, and relational. It is important to note the connection between encouragement and relational aspects of leadership. This relates to the idea of "emotional intelligence" but has a robust set of data supporting it. This is not to say that emotional intelligence lacks research, but as an ongoing and growing field, there are several arenas where its insights could be strengthened.[40]

This theme is present in all three literature reviews[41] and is implied in the communal themes of polycentric structures as well as being required for developing mutual vision and collaboration. It is explicit in the GLOBE study, which uses the label *humane-oriented* to describe the relational dimensions of leadership as important traits for CEOs. And, similar to the literature on polycentric structures, implications abound in the work on governance. It's clear that cooperation and sharing are key aspects of effective leadership in polycentric systems.

The relational theme elicited the fewest responses in the interviews, with only 13 of the 33 interviewees commenting. This could be due to the similarities this trait shares with the communal theme. I kept them distinct because of the uniqueness of their impact as well as the prominence within the literature.

Chris Wright, former chair of the theology working group, noted this quality when answering the question about effective Christian leadership and

---

[39] Tira, 2014.

[40] Mayer, John, Peter Salovey, and David Caruso, "Emotional Intelligence: Theory, Findings and Implications. *Psychological Inquiry*, 2004, 15:3, 197-215.

[41] See Table "Chart of Crossover Themes", 62.

what shaped his leadership style: "John Stott [had] a very strong capacity for friendship. He had great intentionality about developing friends. He didn't just get to know people: he knew their names, children, families and prayed for people. He was very relational. That is an element of effective Christian leadership: warmth and fellowship."[42] Perhaps no one captured this relational theme more adeptly than Ramez Atallah, program chair for Cape Town 2010 and former Lausanne board member. He speaks of the relationships that impacted him and the importance of how we should treat one another:

> During that time, I began my friendship with Leighton Ford who was the youngest trustee of the seminary and that relationship changed my life … Within that context, I have tried to keep my leadership being a people-centered leadership. I lead basically in a pastoral way rather than administrative way and I think that is desperately needed in our very mechanized, organized and systematized world.

> Fruitful kingdom influence is mentoring others in the long term so that you can build into their lives principles of life and leadership that will help them be transforming agents in the next generation. Since I have lived a very long time (I am 72 now) I can look back to my investment in young men and women, some of whom I didn't think would add up to much, and now to see them being influencers within the church and within society. That is the most rewarding experience I have ever experienced in my life and I am continuing to invest in younger people today in the hopes that this multiplication of mentorship will bring fruit in the future as it has in the past.[43]

At least three of the leaders interviewed expressed concerns that the Lausanne Movement had shifted from a relational to an organizational form of leadership. They emphasized the need for more relational, movement-oriented leadership for the future. Many of the others, while never mentioning the organizational aspect, spoke of the crucial importance of relational capital and of fostering trust and friendship over long periods of time. As the interviews progressed over time, these concerns about building the relational bonds started to subside and were superseded by more positive comments. Throughout the interviews, it was made very clear that maintaining relational connectivity was and continues to be a high value.

Given the similarities found between this and the communal theme, further research is encouraged to discover the nuances that are different between them and/or discern if they do, in fact, represent a similar theme overall. For now, I've kept them separate because of how prominently they were distinct within the literature reviews.

---

[42] Wright, Christopher. Interview, 2016.
[43] Atallah, Ramez. Questionnaire, 2018.

Charisma

Charisma is the sixth and final theme, and one that is common to many leadership theories, including this one. [44] The common themes under this umbrella include *charismatic, value-based,* and *spiritual.* Some may find it surprising that these traits are grouped together but, in actuality, *charisma* is defined more broadly when applied to the charismatic leader. Specifically, while charisma of the leader may be obvious, the charisma noted in the research includes depth of character and background and an ethos based on values, as well as a spiritual dimension exhibiting a higher level of consciousness or aspiration. As the GLOBE study noted, these other values were more important in this aspect of leadership than the popular idea of a winsome, charismatic leader. This, coupled with the research from the GLOBE study on Charismatic Leadership Theory, gives further strength to this theme.

By examining the crossover chart (page 62), it is evident that charisma aligns with *mutual vision, innovation,* and *catalyst* in the material on polycentric structures. For polycentric governance, ideas related to empowerment and encouragement are key to charismatic leadership. And, for the GLOBE study, charismatic themes are most prominent.

This theme also drew the most comments from the Lausanne interviews. Nearly everyone – 30 of the 33 people interviewed – commented on the theme of charisma or charismatic leadership. There may be a few reasons for this: 1) given that this is a group of mission leaders, their focus would be heavily spiritual in nature with a reliance on the importance of character; 2) the group has a sense of calling or vision that is driving them; and 3) their giftings may cause them to highlight this dimension. Whatever the reason for such a strong correlation, it is clear that this theme plays a significant role in polycentric leadership.

All of those I interviewed mentioned the spiritual aspects of missional leadership: being biblically based, focusing on character formation, and demonstrating Christ-like servant leadership. Faithfulness and humility are deeply connected to this thread of spirituality. Other more practical attributes relate to the need for vision, passion, and relational competence. Every leader also pointed to a common feature in their life story: God clearly intervening and calling them to ministry. Over and above this aspect of calling was a deep sense of need for the Lord's presence to enable them to serve according to their distinct giftedness. Tira stated, "The Church is yearning for this type of intimacy."[45] In describing his own life story and leadership transition, Chiang referred to how the Lord recently challenged him. He heard the Holy Spirit

---

[44] To more fully understand this leadership theory, look into the research by Shamir, Boaz, Robert House and Michael Arthur. "The Motivational Effects of Charismatic Leadership: A Self-Concept Based Theory," *Organizational Science.* 4:4 1993, 577-594.

[45] Tira, 2014.

whisper to him, "How clean is your soul and can I dwell in it?"[46] Mats Tunehag, former catalyst for business as mission, saw something that deeply fits the Lausanne ethos as a key need in the world. He stated that the world needs leaders "to be like Jesus, who constantly and consistently met the needs of the people who came to him. And most came with physical needs, or with social, legal, or economic issues. Jesus never told anyone they had the wrong kind of need. He met their needs, broadened their horizons, and demonstrated the Kingdom of God."[47] Tunehag was also concerned that the Lausanne Movement retain its focus on calling "The Whole Church to take the Whole Gospel to the Whole World."[48] In essence, by focusing on the concerns that Jesus cares about, leaders embody his values and emulate his character.

One key element to this theme is character. Awuku stated that "Christ-like character as the call of Christian leadership will be our greatest distinguishing mark for both the church and mission today. The world is going through its own crisis of leadership and probably only the outstanding Christ-centered character that stands the test of times will be the most distinguishing."[49] Atallah also highlighted this important aspect of charisma: "The number one priority in the church today is integrity in all levels, financial, sexual, moral and many other ways. The deterioration of commitment to integrity or the lack of our understanding of integrity is threatening the very fabric of the church."[50] Given the crises that multiplied in the church worldwide over the last several years, this is an area where we should also be humble and contrite. The explosion of deep character flaws being exposed should cause us to pause and discern how we can better embody Christ-like leadership in our world today.

Character is certainly key to charismatic leadership. The GLOBE study definitively affirms this. And for mission leaders in particular, spirituality is paramount. Byron Spradlin, catalyst for the arts, emphasizes that "private, personal, intimate, worship walk with the Lord is number one. Powerful public ministry comes from passionate private worship walk with the Lord. If we don't deeply go into this, we won't overcome sensuality, greed, and won't have a strong marriage. Big time spiritual warfare in life and ministry."[51] Pier put it this way: "To me the most important thing in leadership is getting revelation from God. The depth of our influence is in proportion to our intimacy with God. If you are in tune with God, people will trust you even if your ideas are audacious."[52] Sarah Breuel, director for the Younger Leaders Gathering in Jakarta 2016 and current board member, adds:

---

46 Chiang, 2014.
47 Tunehag, Mats. Interview, 2014.
48 Lausanne Website, accessed 2019.
49 Awuku, 2018.
50 Atallah, 2018.
51 Spradlin, Byron, Interview, 2014.
52 Pier, 2019.

[Leadership] falls down to God raising people whose hearts are so given to him. People who are reckless to saying "yes" to Jesus. No challenges are too big for that. Dependency on God! John 15 for me. Abiding the daily life and drawing from the source. Completely dependent on Jesus. The most important thing is dependency on God and abiding in Jesus. Just trust God with every fiber of your being.[53]

Finally, when looking at charisma as a theme, vision is crucial. Butler characterizes this aspect:

Cast vision! You have to believe in your vision and hold out a goal and give them a chance to participate. The more a movement is like Lausanne and WEA, the more it has to define its purpose. The biggest challenge is defining its clarity and vision and focus and then alignment of all its tentacles. Clearly, the leader must go and share their vision and then what the collective impact is: 1+1= 3x5. Unless that leader has that galvanizing conviction. They must say, "This is the beach we're going to take!"[54]

Grace Samson-Song, Lausanne board member, also captured this well: "An effective Christian leader, in my opinion, is someone that is able to engage with various spheres of society, and someone who is solidly grounded in a relationship with God that goes beyond a pulpit, with gravitas enough to challenge and inspire others towards change and transformation."[55] It is obvious that charisma is vital to effective polycentric leadership. Whether it be good character, spiritual inspiration, or casting and carrying out vision, this is a theme that is vitally important to leading well as a mission leader today. Birdsall summarizes many of these comments with his own assessment:

Ministry vision doesn't begin with human initiative but with a divine invitation. Greatness is seen in overcoming obstacles (in perseverance) not accomplishments. People who work out of moral power and authority have been given gifts of leadership, communication, administration, and inspiration. [People who know how] to walk between the two extremes of analysis of paralysis and ready, fire, aim. People who actually know the landscape. [They are] smart and understand what needs to happen and have a plan. [They have the]

---

[53] Breuel, Sarah. Interview, 2018.

[54] Butler, 6 December 2014 interview via Skype. It must be noted here the apparent differences between this statement and the comment by Birdsall below (see comment connected to footnote 67). While at first glance, one sees a divergence between what may appear as top down leadership or charismatic leadership and the qualities of communal, collaborative and freedom; overall Phill's interview and subsequent conversations highlight these other themes. His entire ethos since founding InterDev and serving as the Lausanne Catalyst for Partnership highlights these. Here, in this comment, he is responding to a specific question and merely noting the importance of this theme labeled Charisma.

[55] Samson-Song, Grace. Questionnaire, 2018.

calling, integrity, understand the times, and marshal resources to bring about intended change for good. They create cohesion with freedom. They create excitement because of what we can do together. [They know how] to build rivers and banks and dams to get the water moving and generating power.[56]

Bob Doll, board chair when the interview was conducted, shared this:

Put Christ first. His Word first. Devotion to God. A Godly lifestyle: integrity, honesty, ability to be strategic. The ability to focus and get the organization to focus. Be efficient and effective. Set deadlines, set goals. Don't be just a good relationship person. Pick good people. The ability to raise dollars. Transparency of life ... integrity issue is front and center now. Saw that myself as CEO of Merrill Lynch Investment Managers ... People were watching me all the time. What are the action steps? Metrics and Deadlines. Realism and not unbridled optimism.[57]

These last two voices capture the essence of this theme of charisma and highlight the character, vision, and spiritual sides of the equation. But they go a step further, pointing to some of the other realities, such as the capacity to mobilize, organize, and set the pace for achieving successful outcomes. Many voices have affirmed and confirmed the importance of charisma for polycentric leadership. As the GLOBE study revealed, charisma has more to do with the character and quality of the leader and their leadership than with the charisma of their personality.[58] As leaders within the Global Church family, the charismatic dimension being formed by the fruit of the Spirit, and the humility to listen and learn from others and consider others more highly than oneself, are paramount to those elements of vision-casting at every level in which we lead.

Conclusion

The interviews with Lausanne Movement leaders confirmed that a Polycentric Mission Leadership model that focuses on the six themes identified is worth further investigation.

---

[56] Birdsall, 2015.
[57] Doll, Bob. Interview, 2018.
[58] See p. 83 of Chapter 3 of the House dissertation (1976) as well as House, Robert J. et al. 2014, 268.

6. Toward a New Theoretical Model

Reviewing the Lausanne Movement

The Lausanne Movement has had an important impact on mission history. From its inception as a counterbalance to the ongoing discussions in mission history, particularly with an emphasis on evangelism and subsequently the blending of social elements of the gospel, it has shaped the face of modern evangelical mission reflection and activity.[1] Additionally, the movement drew attention to the peoples of the world who had the least opportunity to hear about Christ with its focus on unreached people groups.[2]

While these milestones may be one of the Lausanne Movement's greatest legacies, Rob Martin, former US director and catalyst for resource mobilization, believes that the real strength of the movement is in the issue groups.[3] 34 priority issues were initially identified during the Pattaya Forum in 2004, and the Cape Town Commitment of 2010 established a road map for pursuing 33 of those pressing missional challenges. While it has been valuable for the movement to affirm the priority of evangelism – the focus of the whole mission of the church, and the importance of unreached peoples – it has also significantly identified many of the critical issues that need to be addressed by the Global Church and mission in the following decade.

In this chapter, I will: 1) examine the movement in light of the research conducted in this study and illuminate some of these findings; 2) touch upon the future of the movement and key changes made post-Cape Town; and 3) describe the key themes discovered within the literature about polycentrism and how they, coupled with the findings from the interviews, highlight an emerging theory for polycentric leadership.

Polycentric Mission Leadership

The Lausanne Movement provided a rich laboratory for testing the idea of a polycentric theory for leadership. In 2000, Lausanne was on the verge of what many thought would be imminent collapse, but by 2004 a new leader brought fresh life to the movement. That era culminated with the Third Lausanne

---

[1] Hunt, Robert. "The History of the Lausanne Movement, 1974-2011." *International Bulletin of Mission Research*, 35:2, April, 2011, 81.
[2] Stott, John. "Twenty Years after Lausanne: Some Personal Reflections." *International Bulletin of Missionary Research*, 19, 2, 1995, 50.
[3] Martin, 2018.

Congress in Cape Town 2010. Shortly thereafter, another era began, ushering in a different leadership dynamic with some younger voices leading the way. Additionally, more leaders were chosen from the Majority World to give shape to the various issue networks.

The research for this study on polycentrism began with the literature reviews in Chapters 2 and 3. In Chapter 2, I reviewed the history of the Lausanne Movement to gain an overview of the background of the research and the operating leadership paradigms used, particularly from 2000–2018. I also examined the history of polycentrism for mission progress, discovering a polycentric development rather than a unidirectional development. Mission history is replete with examples of multipolar progress from various countries and within various regions of the world. Mission progress has often developed through polycentric means rather than from one particular country or region toward another. As Jehu Hanciles aptly points out, "The globalization of Christianity was decidedly polycentric." [4] The implication here is that polycentrism is important to mission progress and has been key to mission history. Building on this concept is Allen Yeh's review of the five congresses, celebrating the centennial year of the Edinburgh 1910 Missionary Conference. Yeh advocates for a Polycentric Missiology, given the research from these five events. He argues that mission today cannot be led or developed adequately without a polycentric framework in mind. Thus, he advocates for a "polycentric missiology", as the title of his book implies. The critiques of both of these concepts (polycentric history and missiology) suggest that further research is imperative. [5] The scholarly research on polycentric history for mission structures is a few decades old, and the work by Yeh is refreshing. This historic backdrop lays the initial foundation for an emerging theory of polycentric leadership. Clearly, there is evidence that mission history has developed in a polycentric fashion and Yeh argues that the future of mission needs to be more polycentric in focus based on the multipolar realities of the world and the outflow of these five congresses.

Building on this foundation, the focus of Chapter 3 was on polycentric structures in the life of missional churches and mission organizations. J.R. Woodward, in his book *Creating a Missional Culture*, suggests a polycentric model for leadership in the local church-based on his understanding of Ephesians 4:7-16. [6] Kirk Franklin comes to a similar conclusion in his thesis, which viewed the structures of the Wycliffe Global Alliance. He developed an emerging model that he calls a "new paradigm for global mission leadership" that uses polycentrism as a key feature. [7] Both Woodward and Franklin advocated for a new approach that strengthens the concept put forth by Yeh:

---

[4] Hanciles, 2008, 29.
[5] Kim, 2017.
[6] Woodward, JR, 2013, 58.
[7] Franklin, 2016.

the need for polycentrism in the future of mission. In Woodward and Franklin's cases, this is the need for a polycentric model of leadership. Although their studies show promise in considering polycentrism as a theory for mission leadership, neither fully describes the concept nor researches the idea as a new theory of leadership. Both do encourage that further studies should be conducted on polycentrism, however, and their studies show promise for considering polycentrism as a theory for mission leadership.

In Chapter 3, I appraised the importance of polycentric governance since the 1950s. At this point, the research began to see a stronger connection to polycentric leadership. The research behind polycentric governance surveys several ecosystems where polycentrism has been successfully operating. One of the key findings is that effective leadership takes place when diverse entities are given the freedom to operate of their own accord without controls from a central governing body.[8] Supplementing this research, Movement Theory was addressed with particular attention to Theodore Esler's research on mission movements.[9] Again, the theoretical constructs within Movement Theory and Network Leadership affirm the emergent findings within the literature.

I continued in Chapter 3 by reviewing the GLOBE study to ascertain if these studies provide evidence of and validity for an emerging theory. As noted in that chapter, the GLOBE study is widely acclaimed for its research and findings. In reviewing their research, six prominent themes surfaced that exist among polycentric leaders: charisma, collaborative, communal, diverse, freedom, and relational. These same traits were evident among the qualitative interviews of movement leaders in the Lausanne Movement.

These six themes comprise an emerging theory of polycentric leadership and are presented in a charted and color-coded format in Chapter 4, which provides a cross-reference identifying where each trait is mentioned in the literature.[10] The data from the qualitative interviews among Lausanne Movement leaders (Chapter 5) supplements these findings, reinforcing their validity as core themes of polycentric leadership.

Conclusions

In discerning this potential theoretical model of Polycentric Mission Leadership, we can draw several conclusions and recommendations.

Lausanne History and Polycentrism

As I look at the Lausanne Movement in light of the research, I return to the questions and proposals posed in my research proposal.[11] The first question

---

[8] Brohm, 2005, 42.

[9] Esler, 2012.

[10] See page 59 above.

[11] See Appendix A for the chart and questions.

intended to answer what within the movement precipitated the need for a Polycentric Mission Leadership model. The movement began with the charismatic leadership of Billy Graham, which highlights one of the key themes found within this study: charisma.[12] However, Graham didn't lead independently; there was always some degree of collaboration.[13] Even from the beginning of the Lausanne Movement, people like John Stott, Jack Dain, and Don Hoke played important roles within the leadership. But few can question the influence of charisma in the development of the movement overall, particularly with the unique presence of Billy Graham. Decades later, when the movement seemed to be at an impasse, some pointed to Doug Birdsall as another charismatic leader who was key to bringing life to a struggling movement.

More recently, as the world has changed and leadership develops across broader sectors, the need for collaboration has become even more important. For example, during a season of Sabbath or break, the movement seemed to being doing well as Menchit Wong, current board chair, aptly described: "Michael [Oh] has been on sabbatical since December and the movement is doing fine."[14] Samuel Chiang, catalyst for orality, also captures the importance of collaboration in leadership adeptly: "[In order to be effective as a leader today] you have to be willingly collaborative."[15]

In terms of governance, the movement made a significant change at the end of Cape Town 2010. Rather than having a loose board of friends working with an executive chairman, the leadership decided to appoint a formal board and accountable CEO. As a backdrop to this change, one of the more intriguing stories is that of the challenge of leadership transition. In his thesis, Birdsall highlighted the challenges around the Manila Congress (1989), which became a key backdrop for his dissertation about conflict and collaboration. At that time, there was a clear problem related to the themes of diversity and freedom, specifically the tensions between Leighton Ford and Thomas Wang.[16] As an East Asian, Wang was accustomed to leading from a Chinese perspective, while the leadership of Lausanne at the time was predominantly Western. East Asian leadership tends to be more hierarchical in nature while Western styles are more democratic. The Lausanne leadership stepped in to restore the status quo, which undermined Wang's leadership, shaming a leader from an honor/shame culture. Former board member Roger Parrott shared:

---

[12] For the value of charisma, see: House, Robert, et al. 2013, xv, 58, 260, 268. See also, Pierson, 2009, 135-149.

[13] For the importance of collaboration see: Bainbridge, 1996, 1997, 3. Also see Addison, 2015, 15.

[14] Wong, Menchit. Interview, 2018.

[15] Chiang, 2014.

[16] See the following looking at freedom as a theme: Morse, 1998, 234. Also: Jones, Candace, Hesterly and Borgatti. 1997, 911-945. Also, Schein, 1985,143-144 and Esler, 2012, 220. On the value of diversity: Yeh, 2016, 38. Also Cattan, 2007.

It was 10 years after the Congress; I was with Thomas [Wang]. And we unpacked it together. "Roger: Why did it have to happen? Why couldn't we work together?" said Wang. International leadership had to break out for it to work together. It didn't come into place until Michael. Doug tried to start it, but Michael was able to move it. It's come a gigantic circle.[17]

After the Manila event, the movement started to lose steam according to a few leaders highlighted earlier in this study. It wasn't that the leaders weren't charismatic or capable, but the movement as a whole lacked momentum. It was at this point that Birdsall was brought in to help lead the movement. His unique strengths in the relational and charismatic themes helped rebuild momentum and take the movement toward the 2010 Congress. Mats Tunehag, catalyst for business as mission, captures what many have mentioned about Birdsall: "[I was] quite impressed with Doug Birdsall. A number of times we didn't see eye to eye, but he got it. Relational, professional, global, people, build community – Doug was outstanding!"[18]

Once again, however, challenges surfaced during the Congress as there was a significant financial issue. Some members felt that the movement had little accountability, as well as little real support, which prompted the shift toward a governance model with more control and less freedom – another of the key themes mentioned for polycentric leadership. Some suggested that the movement relied too much on charisma and seemed less communal or collaborative, two other themes identified this study.[19] This period led to a challenging time for the movement as a whole.

The transition to a new leader was not simple, either. When I first conducted interviews for this research, many doubted the movement overall; however, as time passed, things shifted in a more positive direction. The interview participants appreciate the freedom that the leadership has given them, the collaborative spirit within the movement, and the diversity that the leaders are pursuing.

As part of the methodology for this research, a non-Westerner was asked to read this chapter and provide perspective. Francis Tsui, a Hong Kong-based business leader, was selected to reflect on what he saw.[20] One of his

---

[17] Parrott, 2018.

[18] Tunehag, 2014. For more on the relational theme, see Franklin, Crough and Crough, 2017, 94. Also, Logan, King, and Fischer-Wright, 2008,14.

[19] On communal as a theme see: Schreiter, Robert. "From the Lausanne Movement to Cape Town Commitment." *International Bulletin of Mission Research,* 35:2, April, 2011, 92 and Dahle, 2014, 20-21. Also: Ahn, Kyo Seong. "Korea as an Early Missionary Center." *Polycentric Structures in the History of World Christianity.* Berlin: Harrassowitz Verlag, 2014, 100 and Scholte, 2004.

[20] Francis Tsui, as mentioned in Chapter 4, is a board member of Asian Access but someone who has been deeply involved in mission for several years as the director of Asian Outreach and board chair for CMS Asia. He also holds a Ph.D. in East Asian History with graduate degrees from both Hong Kong and the United States. He is

observations relates to encouraging mission movements to go even further into polycentric leadership. In walking with the Chinese church mission movements, he saw the angst of their willingness to work with outsiders and especially Western dominate groups:

> I observe that the Chinese church is still struggling in how to situate itself [in] its role in global mission. How close they should work with established West-based mission movements and organizations (and infrastructure), or should they develop their own missiology, infrastructure, and mechanism? There are still many differing opinions on both sides of the arguments.

He follows this astute observation by asking the following question:

> The China mission vision 2030[21] ... can it fit into the polycentric model of mission development in the non-Chinese world, or in the broader Lausanne vision? It is not about what and how Lausanne may like to lead/serve, but, rather, how the Chinese church might like to drive. Maybe there, in fact, is a wider application of polycentrism in missional development.[22]

Doug McConnell, Professor at Fuller Seminary, amplified this concern, stating,

> This is a key point. It isn't about what LCWE offers; it is about what the church receives. This is a perennial problem. I noted it first leading up to and following Lausanne II as a mission director and a member of a pastoral team in Melbourne, AUS. LCWE was, at best, a helpful ancillary network to our work in the church and the broader work of our mission.[23]

For Lausanne to go deeper in serving the Global Church, developing an even broader Polycentric Mission Leadership model would serve them well. They are making good strides and, through involving more diversity in the leadership systems, their effectiveness in truly serving the church worldwide will be enhanced.

Tsui raises some important questions about polycentrism and Western dominance. He further posed:

> Does being polycentric mean less Western dependent? I think the jury is still out on that. Most of those non-Western leaders are still closely linked and related to [the West], and most of these non-Western leaders received their education and

---

currently a D.Min. student at Fuller Seminary focusing on Business as Mission and has been involved with the Lausanne Movement.

[21] Mission 2030 is a vision from the modern Chinese Church to send 20,000 missionaries from China to other unreached nations by the year 2030 – https://www.chinasource.org/blog/posts/mission-china-2030-in-korea.

[22] Reflections provided via email on 1 December 2019.

[23] McConnell, C. Douglas, Response on 3 December 2019.

training in Western or somewhat old Christendom contexts. Therefore, being polycentric could be different from being non-Western- centric.

This is a very important observation and one that I hear frequently as a mission leader. While not all of the non-Western leaders I interviewed for this study were educated in the West, many of them were. Ideally, as this study indicates, a broader alliance of leaders should be active in the ecosystems of mission leadership. For Lausanne and other mission organizations and movements, this is an area worthy of close examination. For a truly polycentric form of mission leadership to emerge, local and regional leaders will be empowered and foster their own initiatives before and as they engage the global contexts. In this way, the mission world will begin to see a fuller spectrum of indigeneity expressed which will better inform the global frameworks of world mission and lead to more insightful global engagement in mission overall.

The transition to a formal leadership structure within the Lausanne Movement also received mixed reviews. Parrott mentioned that the move created some backlash coming out of the Congress. However, he clarified that the new model has proven to be effective. In his perspective, "We really built the structure around the people. You have an empowered board and clear delegation to the CEO."[24] Ram Gidoomal, the chairman during the shift, stated, "[This was an] all-new culture for Lausanne. Many didn't understand [the move] and [the] why behind it."[25]

Similarly, Byron Spradlin, catalyst for the arts, had this to say about the leadership ecosystem: "Structured leadership initiators (Bennett is doing a great job of facilitating senior associates) – [b]ut [the] verdict is out on integration between International Deputy Directors and Senior Associates, and frankly I haven't seen this working well yet." He also suggested, "We don't know how the younger generation will respond and how well the old guard can give up the reigns. [I have] more questions than answers on this but happy to ride the wave and see and get it moving."[26]

The key question here, especially in light of the literature on polycentric governance, is how much freedom will be given for the movement to self-organize, create, and lead in an entrepreneurial fashion.[27] There are signs of progress. The momentum around the Younger Leader Networks in Lausanne seems to be strong today and some of the more recent interviewees had more positive responses. Menchit Wong, current board chair, commended the board, recognizing that, "It's a very collegial discussion, not top-down. You don't feel any stress. We're making decisions together. Very democratic,

---

[24] Parrott, 2018.
[25] Gidoomal, 2015.
[26] Spradlin, Byron. Interview 2014.
[27] Aligica and Tarko, 2012, 2.

empowering." She sees that, "The hope of Lausanne is the development of younger leaders. Michael is being intentional about younger leaders. The strategy [requires] younger leaders. To the extent that they empower younger leaders [Lausanne's future will be bright]."[28]

Speaking about these changes, Bob Doll, the recent chairman, admits, "The structure is okay, but it's not solved all the problems. The reason is how well the leaders are connected. We are making progress, but we are not there yet."[29] Despite this structural change, Phill Butler believes that the formal structure will not change the character of the collaborative nature of the movement. It's simply a structure to help with efficiency. His response was simple: "Lausanne doesn't have a CEO even if that title exists." Butler went on to note how he had recommended to Doug Birdsall that they call David Bennett a chief collaboration officer, which helps bolster a key theme from this study.[30] However, as Spradlin noted above, the shift toward a more formal structure could pose a challenge for the longer-term viability of the Lausanne Movement. The findings from this research strongly assert that a more polycentric structure – one that has further diversity engaged at all levels of leadership – is essential. The questions remain: *Is Butler's assessment correct? Will the formal leadership structure, in an effort to bring further efficiency, still foster the fullness of a collaborative, polycentric model, or will it inhibit the freedom necessary to see effective missional movements thrive? Or, will Tira's comment that they must be careful not to weaken the movement by having an organization run by a CEO become a challenge?* These are challenges that require keen relational skills, as highlighted in the polycentric theoretical model. The balance of the relationships alongside the efficiency of work will be an important one going forward. As this study reveals, relationships are king and, when healthy, they can produce healthy, fruitful witness and mission.

Related to this question is what is developed later in this chapter about the way God leads through the Trinity and seeing that as a potential polycentric model throughout scripture. This is a leadership approach that deserves further research. Lesslie Newbigin initiated some of these ideas through advocating for a Trinitarian missiology and it was highlighted to some degree by Samuel Chiang, J.R. Woodward, and especially Kirk Franklin, in this study.[31] Does the shift Lausanne has made illuminate these questions further? Will the move toward a formal structure strengthen or weaken a more Trinitarian approach to leadership within the *Missio Dei*?

---

[28] Wong, 2018.

[29] Doll, 2018.

[30] Butler, 2019.

[31] See the following pages to see the engagement: Newbigin, 1995, 111, 114; Chiang, 2014, 164, Woodward, 2013, 132, and Franklin, 2016, 72, 82, 105, 107, and 155. Further discussion comes up later in this chapter as well as on 109, 118 and 119.

My proposition was that leadership prior to Cape Town 2010 relied more on charisma than on collaboration. It does appear that there was a distinctive shift toward a more collaborative, interdependent model of leadership, with leadership transitions beginning at Manila, but more evident following Cape Town. The question about the formalized structure notwithstanding, many of the leaders shared encouraging words about the growing diversity of the network leadership systems since the Cape Town Congress. Best illustrating this shift are the comments by Nana Yaw Offei Awuku:

> Nobody anywhere should set the agenda for the global church today. It must be a collaborative effort. What I would say is encouraging is that some of the barriers to leadership collaboration that came from colonial heritage have been eroded to a very large extent. We have a new generation who are excited to work together. That's huge!
>
> I've experienced, in personal friendship and partnerships, a growing openness of the church in the Global North saying we need to do this together. The growing partnership for global mission as the church becomes more and more global, both in representation and its membership, is a key thing. From the perspective of the handling of scripture, I am seeing more and more, in global conferences, the desire of global planning teams to have the multiple representation, to have the voices of church leaders around the world.
>
> When you say the movement, nothing describes it more than its strength in collaborating for global mission. All of us must do it together. No one can do it alone.[32]

Awuku's reflections are an encouraging sign for the movement and a hopeful model for the future. If Lausanne is able to freely empower movement leaders to lead their networks without top-down controls or hindrances from the formal structure, leaders will more ably flourish and likely produce more entrepreneurial missional endeavors in the future. If, however, the concerns of Spradlin and Tira about the governance becoming a hindrance arise, this will stifle movement leaders and decrease Lausanne's missional effectiveness. It is important for the Lausanne leadership community as a whole to safeguard these freedoms, discern where guidelines are hampering the mission, and foster the communal and collaborative spirit to keep the momentum going.[33] As they listen to God in community, they can monitor these dangers and foster the entrepreneurial spirit that will help the movement flourish.

---

[32] Awuku, 2018.
[33] The Lausanne Mission and Vision Statements, 2020.

Polycentrism in Missiology and Mission History

The second research question from my original chapter explored the findings from the studies on missiology and mission history. Following this question, I proposed that mission history and missiology reveal more polycentric development than has typically been suggested and that leadership exhibited more transnational and global development with more cooperation and collegial approaches.

The study assessed Allen Yeh's advocacy for Polycentric Missiology through the lens of the historic centennial gatherings in 2010 and 2012. Yeh was one of the few people who actually attended all five congresses, noting their strengths and contributions to mission strategy as well as their weaknesses. He concluded that no single event could fully represent the heritage stemming back to Edinburgh 1910. Given the multipolar, complex, transnational nature of mission today, mission strategy had moved from "everyone to everywhere" and required a Polycentric Missiology to more ably strategize in mission for this era. Implicit in his research is that not only mission, but also mission leadership, needs to operate in a more polycentric fashion.[34]

This implicit argument can also be found in the research by the Munich School of World Christianity, which has been exploring the idea of polycentric structures in mission history for a few decades. Their findings reveal that mission developed from various centers of influence rather than unidirectionally from one nation to another or from one mission leader or agency to a particular country. In many cases, the mission developed within the country itself via influences from globalization through business dealings or NGO leadership cross-pollination between countries and regions. The data, for polycentric leadership in particular, is based more on implication rather than concrete evidence. It's plausible that all of these developments were led by inspired individuals working in isolation from one another. While that may be true in many cases, in other situations it was clearly polycentric in its formation, particularly in the development of the YMCA's influence in East Asia.[35]

Polycentric governance models by Elinor Ostrom and the Bloomington School at Indiana University were consulted to provide credibility to this emerging idea.[36] Their research uncovered a significant amount of data that supports polycentric governance principles. Most notable is the notion or theme of freedom. While this theme is seen throughout the literature, it found the strongest application within the governance literature and therefore

---

[34] Yeh, 2016, 38.

[35] To see the polycentric, or as some might argue multipolar, aspects of the YMCA: Ng, 2014, 133. Also: Hermann, 2014, 202. Lehmann, 2014, 378.

[36] Ostrom, Elinor. *Governing the Commons: The Evolution of Institutions for Collective Action.* Cambridge: Cambridge University Press, 1990.

becomes a crucial theme for Polycentric Mission Leadership. In the next section I provide an overview of a few of the emerging models reviewed in Chapter 4 with a comparison to the GLOBE study findings.

Polycentrism in Mission Structures

When reviewing mission structures and the motivation for employing them, the emergence of a polycentric approach for mission leadership was discovered. Two hypotheses were suggested:

1. Polycentrism provides a stronger leadership paradigm for leading missional endeavors in an interdependent, globally networked world.
2. The Lausanne Movement is shifting to a more polycentric leadership structure as observed in the shift from statist to polycentric models and from state-focused (Westphalian) leadership to multilayered and diffuse forms of governance. The state-focused model had all decisions being made from a central core whereas polycentric leadership pushes decisions to the ground levels of operation.

This led to the following proposition:

Leading in an era of globalization requires a broader array of voices (leaders) representing local and regional constituencies who are empowered to self-organize within complex, adaptive, and self-regulating systems.

The research was based on Woodward's theological framework for missional church leadership based on the five-fold gifts of ministry seen in Ephesians. He explored polycentrism to augment his idea, affirming that Paul's missional leadership approach would function well in today's world.[37]

Woodward's ideas were supplemented by Franklin's thesis about a new paradigm for mission leadership encompassing several elements, including polycentrism. Franklin used a paradigm change theory to review these elements within the Wycliffe Global Alliance, arguing that mission structures need to adapt to a postmodern, global reality. He surmised that mission structures have become overly Western and tied to past institutional models and proposed that the missional leadership approach from Woodward is a better model. Elements in his new paradigm include: 1) theological conceptions of the *Missio Dei,* including a view of God in a Trinitarian leadership ecosystem; 2) globalization; 3) Paradigm Shift Theory; 4) polycentrism; 5) spiritual leadership; and 6) the Wycliffe Global Alliance case study.[38]

Franklin builds on Woodward's concepts, but the real strength of a polycentric leadership model is found in the decades-long research in

---

[37] Woodward, 2013, 58.
[38] Franklin, Crough and Crough, 2017, 217.

polycentric governance. It was at this point that I identified the themes for an emerging theoretical model of polycentric leadership.

During the course of the research, it was fortuitous that the World Evangelical Alliance held its Mission Commission gathering in Panama in 2016. Remarkably, the theme for their gathering was polycentrism because these paradigms were becoming more prominent in mission leadership. They recognized:

> The notions of polycentric mission and "mission from everywhere to everywhere", these closely-related ideas point to the relativising of all centres of influence and power in light of the claims of the cross and of Christ. This extends over all competing loyalties, whether ethnic, cultural, national, political, generational, denominational, or organisational, and offers a re-centering of a united polyphonic missional conversation.[39]

These remarks affirm the ideology presented by Yeh in his research about the five congresses in 2010 and 2012.

What emerged in the review of these mission structures was the essence of a polycentric leadership hypothesis that encompasses the six themes that are culled from the literature on polycentrism and magnified in the interviews conducted with Lausanne Movement leaders. The data affirmed the direction of the first hypothesis – that polycentrism offers a stronger model for effective mission leadership in the world today. The findings support the proposition asserted: that leading in a global era requires a broader array of perspectives who should be empowered and given freedom to lead within their own spheres of influence.

This hypothesis gained further credibility when compared to the GLOBE study of CEOs working in global environments. That study revealed several key traits manifest in global leaders, many of which parallel the findings about polycentric leadership.[40] These common attributes became the core of my research on Polycentric Leadership Theory and were tested among the Lausanne Movement leaders.

Implications for Mission Leadership

This research reveals an emerging theoretical model for global leadership. Various aspects of this model for polycentric leadership can be seen in the traits from the GLOBE study. For instance, the GLOBE study highlights charismatic leadership as one of its key traits and this form of leadership has been studied for many years.[41] Likewise, there are elements within this

---

[39] World Evangelical Alliance held its Mission Commission gathering in Panama, 2016 theme.

[40] House, Hanges, Javidian, Dorfmann and Sulley du Luque. 2013, 210.

[41] See Chapter 3. Also, House, Robert et al. 2013, xv, 58, 260, 268.

emerging theory on polycentrism that correlate with findings from other theories on leadership and from the material on leading social movements.[42]

Unique to this model, however, is the synthesis of leadership themes making up the polycentric model. The work of Woodward and Franklin in highlighting polycentrism as an idea has merit. In this study, the models they have advocated for are taken to a deeper level through the development of key themes making up the theory. As mentioned above, when gathering the insights from the variety of reviews on polycentrism and mission movements, six themes emerged in the literature. When compared with the GLOBE study, these themes are amplified and given further validity due to the GLOBE study's strength as a model. Finally, the Lausanne Movement interviews further strengthened these findings by confirming the concepts present within the emerging theory.

In Chapter 4, I reviewed the polycentric leadership model using the conceptual framework advanced by Northouse. In this, I described the strengths and weaknesses of this model and, even though it was premature to establish a theory, other emerging models provided further support for this concept. The Lausanne interviews strengthened the emergent model, providing evidence that the six themes are present and important for leading in the current environment.

Mission leaders can review these themes in light of their own approaches to leadership and discover their pertinence. In addition, this study suggests that further research could be conducted to amplify the findings and strengthen the viability of a theory. Polycentrism is trending for a number of disciplines today, including governance, mission history, missiology, and praxis. And, with this trendline so prevalent, a deeper look at polycentric leadership is imperative. In fact, there is enough credence to these findings that the scope of this research should move beyond that of mission leaders to the discipline of leadership studies in general. Other primary theories in leadership studies have yet to adequately address issues of polycentricity, issues that remain important in the global environment in which the world operates today. The GLOBE study is an admirable effort toward that end, but these findings related to polycentrism unveil a set of themes that offer a new vantage point for leadership study and praxis.

The GLOBE study, reviewed by Northouse under the rubric of "Culture and Leadership", lacks an important dimension found in this study related to polycentric governance.[43] In these governance studies, the concept of self-governance or what I have labeled *freedom* is crucial for effective governance. This component to leading well in a global setting is imperative and yet it is not well documented for global leadership or what the GLOBE study referred

---

[42] See Chapter 3 on Social Movements. See also Chapter 4 for other similarities with leadership theories.

[43] Northouse, 2013, 7530-8176.

to as "Culture and Leadership". In addition, the GLOBE study does not provide a strong data set related to the importance of diversity. In contrast, this study of polycentric leadership has many examples recognizing the importance of diversity, both in the literary sources as well as the interviews. Of course, the GLOBE study does focus on a wide array of cultures and geographical locations, so perhaps the concept of diversity is assumed or implied.

Other findings in this study align with leadership theories that are well documented. Both the GLOBE study and the studies on transformational leadership and charismatic leadership confirm the value of charisma. [44] Similarly, the findings from this study on collaboration and communal themes pair well with team leadership and servant leadership. [45] In addition, Contingency Theory and situational approaches resonate with findings on freedom and adaptive models, all of which signal the necessity of leading well across multiple locations as well as from a wide variety of perspectives.[46] What is lacking, however, particularly for global leadership, is a comprehensive synthesis of the important traits, behaviors, and operating principles or systems that make up a polycentric model of leadership.

Toward a Stronger Global Leadership Model

As I reflect on these findings in light of current mission leadership, I believe that this study offers a stronger model for effective global leadership. In a world that is ever-changing, with what appears to be increasing polarization, effective spiritual leadership is paramount. A number of helpful resources are available to mission leaders, including a recent book release by my dissertation advisor, Doug McConnell, as well as the book following Franklin's dissertation. [47] Three of these resources (McConnell, Lingenfelter, and Plueddemann) provide substantive spiritual and cultural insights for leadership today. The fourth, Franklin's study, provides a fresh model drawing from missional church studies.

Adding depth to these studies is the ongoing research on global leadership in the GLOBE study. That series of studies has a strong data set verifying a number of important traits that effective leaders embody. This dissertation adds value to these studies for mission leaders by building on these resources, adding further perspective from the ongoing studies on polycentrism as well as social movements. The combination of cultural insights from the studies by

---

[44] Northouse, 3813-4363.
[45] Northouse, 5708ff. for Team Leadership and 4438ff for Servant Leadership.
[46] Northouse, 2237ff. for Situational Approach and 2682ff. for Contingency Theory. See also Heifitz, Linskey and Grashow. 2009.
[47] McConnell, Douglas. *Cultural Insights for Christian Leaders*. Grand Rapids, MI: Baker, 2018, Franklin, Crough, and Crough, 2017. The study also reviewed a few other excellent studies as background material: Lingenfelter, 2008. Plueddemann, James. *Leading Across Cultures*. Downers Grove, IL: IVP Academic, 2012.

mission leaders and academics, alongside the findings from polycentrism and the Lausanne leaders' interviews, as well the GLOBE study, reveal a viable model of leadership for mission leaders to examine and practice.

Mission leaders would benefit if they applied these findings to their praxis of leading in mission. For example, many missions today are still operating in a paradigm similar to what Stanley McChrystal described in his review of the modern US military. They have become institutional in approach rather than adaptive. The findings from polycentric governance about self-governance and freedom of local leadership as part of the model can be particularly helpful. As Franklin has learned from the WGA, empowering the various centers of influence and diverse array of peoples within a movement can lead to enhanced decision-making and more effective operations.

My research also highlights a polycentric model to better empower mission leaders throughout movements and networks. By leaning further into the diversity of God's provision of leaders and their cultural wisdom, a movement can thrive. The Lausanne Movement is moving in that direction, which is encouraging to leaders within the movement. In the mission I serve, Asian Access, we have been experimenting with this polycentric model for the past seven or eight years and have seen good results. Global leaders feel more empowered and have greater ownership of the movement as a whole. Given that they are all volunteers, this is crucial for our success as a mission.[48] Each of them, as well as the regions they represent, play an important role in the movement and their voice is given a platform. The world needs to hear their voices because they have wisdom that is not being heard, which is why we launched a new series called Eastern Voices.[49] The platforming of global voices is vital for God's kingdom. At the end of time, the nations will unite worshipping God, showcasing the ideals Christ has for the life of the church.[50] Just as God's main purpose in choosing Israel was so they could be a light to the nations, in the same way, the *Missio Dei* was intended to reach every nation, tongue, and tribe.[51]

Volunteerism, as referenced in Chapter 2, is a topic that should be researched in relation to polycentric leadership. While it did not surface as a key theme throughout the literature on polycentrism, it does appear in the literature related to social and mission movements. Given that both Asian Access and the Lausanne Movement are led in large part by volunteers, this is an area deserving of further study.[52]

---

[48] See Chapter 4 for further information on volunteers with Asian Access. See Chapter 1 for an inference related to the Lausanne Movement.

[49] Becchetti, Noel.*Eastern Voices: Insight, Perspective and Vision from Kingdom Leaders in their own Voices*. Asian Access, 2017.

[50] See Revelation 5:9-14 and 7:9-17.

[51] See Isaiah 49:6 and 51:4 as well as Matthew 24:14 and 28:18-20.

[52] See 90-96 for the references related to Social and Mission Movements, particularly looking at the work of Schein, Walls and Esler.

MissioNexus, a network of North American mission leaders, appreciated the merits of this polycentric approach and decided to publish early lessons from the model.[53] If mission leaders employ this collaborative, communal model, it should enhance their effectiveness. If they capitalize on the vast diversity of perspectives, regional outlooks, and local expressions within their networks and movements, they would better empower those God has gifted within their spheres of influence, fully deploying them to achieve their mission, vision, and goals. Just as Asian Access has profited from applying the polycentric model, I'm convinced other mission leaders and organizations could as well.

Giving freedom to each leader, region, and country to make decisions in their own settings allows the adaptive and creative energy to flow based on the local context and situation. This move, at least by Asian Access, has engendered deep levels of trust and fostered a level of volunteer ownership like I have never seen before. The community unites as these relationships are fostered and that unity extends to the movement as a whole. It's not something that just operates on a local level. Rather, this spirit pervades the entirety of our movement. Miroslav Volf speaks of the value of diffusion of power and unity in diversity: "With regard to the distribution of power, one can distinguish between symmetrical-polycentric and asymmetrical-monocentric models; with regard to cohesion, one can distinguish between coerced and freely affirmed integration."[54] As mission leaders empower the various centers of gravity in their networks and organizations, deeper levels of ownership are fostered, leading to greater unity in the diversity and effectiveness in mission.

Just as the Wycliffe Global Alliance and Asian Access have experienced success in applying polycentric approaches, I believe this study can be helpful to the Lausanne Movement. They have clearly made strides toward a more polycentric model of leadership. The shift to a formal board and CEO could have proven catastrophic, but they appear to remain focused on leading as a movement. The more they can empower the leaders in their networks, the more effective they will become. Hopefully, the latest Mission Commission gathering for the WEA will prove equally instructive as they pursue a more polycentric nature of mission for the future.

As mentioned in Chapter 2, success for mission leaders today hinges on our dependence on the ideal polycentric leader: God the Father, Jesus the Son, and the Holy Spirit. It is in their Trinitarian example that this polycentric model draws its greatest strength.[55] As the three Persons of the Trinity collaborate in

---

[53] Handley, Joseph. "Leading Mission Movements." *EMQ (Evangelical Missions Quarterly),* 2018, 20-27.
[54] Volf, Miroslav. *After our Likeness: The Church as the Image of the Trinity.* Grand Rapids, MI, Eerdmans, 1998, 236.
[55] Woodward and Franklin cover the idea and it is highlighted with Newbigin and Chiang.

communal fashion and empower the diversity of their personalities, using their gifts in relationship with one another, and free one another to lead, their charisma inspires a generation of mission leaders to follow.[56] It is from this charisma that leaders draw their strength and wisdom, knowing that only in being connected to the vine can we bear much fruit.

This Trinitarian, biblical perspective adds a unique dimension to polycentric leadership. Just as the Father, Son, and Holy Spirit lead in a communal fashion, and as scriptures provide examples of communal forms of leadership and leadership across different regions and cities, we as mission leaders can continue in this stream by leading polycentrically. Ultimately, it is God who directs our vision and leads the way, and his approach embodies these six themes. His model is one we can emulate as we follow his lead and provide leadership in the realms that he has appointed for us to serve. As we become more polycentric in leadership, we can become more like Christ, the Good Shepherd and Servant Leader.

Further Areas of Study

In Chapter 4, I suggested a few areas that would profit from extended research. [57] It would be useful to review other examples of polycentric leadership models to explore the new theory. Given that WEA's Mission Commission has advocated for Polycentric Missiology, it would be useful to examine other models than the ones reviewed in this research. Providing further evidence would fill in the gaps this dissertation discovered and possibly lead to developing a new theory of leadership. In addition to the arena of mission, the themes uncovered in this research could be applied across a variety of platforms to determine if the theory may be valid beyond the framework of mission movements. Woodward's model from churches could be useful should further studies be conducted. Likewise, the themes could be explored within the broader array of NGOs and even business and government platforms.

I also suggest developing a tool to more effectively measure the presence of these themes within various platforms. A research tool similar to the one used by the GLOBE study could provide further reliability to the model. That tool took a more quantitative approach to measurement, and if something like that could be applied to this theoretical model for Polycentric Mission Leadership, then polycentric leadership in general would prove useful.

Continuing to use the Northouse approach to analyze leadership theories would also be useful as further polycentric models become more prevalent. With new models on the horizon, the theoretical model of a polycentric leadership theory can be explored to a greater degree.

---

[56] See John 10:38.
[57] See 122-124 above for a list of these suggestions.

It would be helpful to further define the themes discovered in this research as well. One of the weaknesses in the GLOBE study was the vagueness of the traits they discovered. Similarly, with polycentric leadership themes, the same critique offered by the Northouse approach could be applied. Clarifying the themes discovered in Polycentric Mission Leadership would prove useful in the discovery of a new leadership theory.

As noted above, I only briefly touched upon volunteerism as a key component to Polycentric Mission Leadership. This is an area deserving more attention because it does appear in the social movement literature. And, as highlighted above, both the Lausanne Movement and Asian Access rely heavily on volunteers. Likewise, Andrew Walls noted that missionary societies in general are basically volunteer organizations.[58] Given the importance of volunteerism, studying this component would contribute to the validity of a polycentric theory for leadership.

Finally, it would be beneficial to explore the Trinity as a model for leadership. Lesslie Newbigin set out some excellent ideas related to Trinitarian mission, which could be instructive for mission movements.[59] My research just lightly touched on these aspects related to Polycentric Mission Leadership. This theological and missiological research could uncover important findings, helping refine the Polycentric Mission Leadership theoretical model.

---

[58] Walls, 1996, 80.
[59] Newbigin, 1995, 29, 65.

Bibliography

Addison, Steve. 2015. *Pioneering Movement: Leadership that Multiplies Disciples and Churches*. Downers Grove, IL: IVP Books.

Adler, N. J., and Bartholomew, S. 1992. *Managing Globally Competent People. Academy of Management Executive*, 6, 1992, 52–65.

Adogame, Afe. 2014. "African 'Retro-Mission' in Europe." Koschorke, Klaus and Hermann, Adrian. Polycentric Structures in the History of World Christianity. Polyzentrische Strukturen in der Geschichte des Weltchristentums. Berlin: Harrassowitz Verlag.

Ahn, Kyo Seong. 2014. "Korea as an Early Missionary Center." Polycentric Structures in the History of World Christianity. Polyzentrische Strukturen in der Geschichte des Weltchristentums. Berlin: Harrassowitz Verlag.

Allen, Roland. 1927. *Mission Activities Considered in Relation to the Manifestation of the Spirit.* London: World Dominion, Press.

Aligica, Paul D. and Vlad Tarko. 2012. *Governance: An International Journal of Policy, Administration, and Institutions*, Vol. 25, No. 2, April, 2012.

Asian Access Vision and Mission Statements. 2019. https://www.asianaccess.org/about2/vision-and-mission (accessed 25 February, 2020).

Atallah, Ramez. 2018. Program chair for Cape Town 2010 and Lausanne board member. 16 May 2018 emailed questionnaire.

_____. 2000. *The Lausanne Movement: A Range of Perspectives*. Eugene, OR: Wipf & Stock.

Atkinson, Robert. 1998. *The Life Story Interview*. Thousand Oaks, CA: Sage Publications.

Avolio, B. J., Walumbwa, F. O., & Weber, T. J. 2009. "Leadership: Current Theories, Research, and Future Directions." *Annual Review of Psychology*, 60, 2009, 421–449.

Awuku, Nana Yaw Offei. 2018. 30, October 2018 interview via Skype. Global Associate Director for Generations with the Lausanne Movement and Senior Management for Scripture Union Ghana.

Bainbridge, William Sims. 1996. *The Sociology of Religious Movements*. New York: Routledge, 1996.

Balia, Daryl M. and Kirsteen Kim. 2010. *Witnessing to Christ Today*. Oxford: Regnum.

Banks, Richard, Bernice Ledbetter and David C. Greenhalgh. 2016. *Reviewing Leadership*. 2nd ed. Grand Rapids, MI: Baker.

Barbour, R. 2007. *Doing Focus Groups*. Thousand Oaks, CA: Sage.

Bass, Bernard M. 1985. *Leadership and Performance Beyond Expectations*. New York: Free Press.

_____. 1990. "From Transactional to Transformational Leadership: Learning to Share the Vision". *Organizational Dynamics*. 18 (3), 1990, 19–31.

_____. 2008. *The Bass Handbook of Leadership*. New York: Free Press.

Bass, Bernard M., and Ralph Melvin Stogdill. 1981. *Stogdill's Handbook of Leadership: A Survey of Theory and Research*. Rev. and expanded ed. New York: Free Press.

Bataillard, Anne-Christine. 2019. Former catalyst for children and evangelism. 28, May 2019 interview via Skype

Becchetti, Noel. 2017. *Eastern Voices: Insight, Perspective and Vision from Kingdom Leaders in Their Own Voices*. Asian Access.

Beford-Strohm, Heinrich. 2014. "Global Christianity as the Horizon of Ecclesial Practice." Koschorke, Klaus and Hermann, Adrian. *Polycentric Structures in the History of World Christianity*. Berlin: Harrassowitz Verlag.

Bellofatto, Gina A. 2011. Review of 2010 Boston: The Changing Contours of World Mission and Christianity. *MissioNexus*. https://missionexus.org/review-of-2010boston-the-changing-contours-of-world-mission-and-christianity/ (accessed 15 November 2015).

Bendor-Samuel, Paul. 2017. "Foreword." In Franklin, Kirk, Dave Crough, and Deborah Crough. *Towards Global Missional Leadership: A Journey through Leadership Paradigm Shift in the Mission of God*. Oxford: Regnum, 11.

Bennett, David William. 2004. *Metaphors of Ministry: Biblical Images for Leaders and Followers*. Eugene, OR: Wipf and Stock.

Bennett, David. 2019. "Global Associate Director for Collaboration and Content." Observation offered on 17 October 2019.

Bennis, W. G., and Nanus, B. 1985. *Leaders: The Strategies for taking Charge*. New York: Harper and Row.

Bennis, Warren and Robert Thomas. 2002. *Geeks and Geezers: How Era, Values and Defining Moments Shape Leaders*. Boston, MA: Harvard Business School Press.

Bernard, H. Russell. 2011. *Research Methods in Anthropology: Qualitative and Quantitative Methods*. Walnut Creek, CA: AltaMira Press.

Bi-Annual Lausanne International Leadership Meeting, Budapest – 2007, Vol. 1.

Birdsall, Doug. 2013. *Conflict and Collaboration: A Narrative History and Analysis of the Interface Between the Lausanne Committee for World Evangelization and the World Evangelical Fellowship, the International Fellowship of Evangelical Mission Theologians, and the AD 2000 Movement*. Ph.D. Oxford Centre for Mission Studies/Middlesex University.

_____. 2014. "Lausanne '74 Stewarding the Legacy" *Lausanne Global Analysis,* Vol 3, Issue 4, July 2014.

_____. 2015. Former Executive Chair. 11 February 2015 interview in El Segundo, CA.

Blumer, H. 1969. *Symbolic Interactionism: Perspective and Method.* Berkeley, CA: University of California Press, 99.

Boff, Leonard. 1988. *Trinity and Society.* Maryknoll, NY: Orbis.

Bosch, David. 1991. *Transforming Mission: Paradigm Shifts in Theology of Mission.* Maryknoll, NY: Orbis.

Bowen, G.L, Martin, J.A., Mancini, J.A. and Nelson, J.P. 2000. *Community Capacity: Antecedents and Consequences,* viewed 15 March 2014, from http://www.fcs.uga.edu/cfd/fcrlweb/docs/ccb/2000_Bowen_Martin_Manc ini_Nelson.pdf.

Bowers, Esme. Board of Directors, Lausanne Movement. 2018. 29 October interview via Skype

Branson, Mark Lau. 2004. *Memories Hopes and Conversations: Appreciative Enquiry and Congregational Change.* Lanham, MD: Rowman and Littlefield.

Breuel, Sarah. 2018. Board Member. Director for the Younger Leaders Gathering and current board member. 15 October interview via Skype.

Brewen, Kester. 2007. *Signs of Emergence: A Vision for Church That Is Organic/Networked/Decentralized/Bottom-up/Communal/Flexible {Always Evolving}* Grand Rapids, MI: Baker.

Brohm, René. 2005. Polycentric Order in Organizations: a dialogue between Michael Polanyi and IT-consultants on knowledge, morality, and organization. Erasmus Research Institute of Management (ERIM). RSM Erasmus University / Erasmus School of Economics Erasmus University Rotterdam.

Brown, Ed. 2014. Catalyst for Creation Care. 2 December interview via Skype

Burns, James MacGregor. 1978. *Leadership.* London: Harper Collins.

Butler, Phill. 2014. Catalyst for Partnership and founder of many Collaborative Mission Efforts today. 6 December interview via Skype

Cameron, Julia. 2014. "John Stott and the Lausanne Movement: A Formative Influence." *The Lausanne Movement: A Range of Perspectives*: ed. Dahle, Lars and Margunn Serigstad Dahle along with Knud Jørgensen. Oxford: Regnum.

Campbell, J. L. 2002. "Where do We Stand? Common Mechanisms in Organizations and Social Movements Research." Social Movements and Organization Theory Conference. Ann Arbor, MI.

Cape Town Commitment, The. 2010. https://www.lausanne.org/content/ctc/ctcommitment (accessed 13 February 2020).

Carey, William. 2010. *An Enquiry into the Obligation of Christians to use Means for the Conversion of the Heathens.* Whitefish, MT: Kessenger Publications.

Cattan, Nadine.2007. *Cities and Networks in Europe: A Critical Approach to Polycentrism.* Esher: John Libbey Eurotext.

Chan, A. 2005. "Authentic leadership measurement and development: Challenges and suggestions." In W. L. Gardner, B. J. Avolio, and F. O. Walumbwa, eds. *Authentic leadership Theory and Practice: Origins, Effects, and Development.* Oxford: Elsevier Science.

Chapman, Alister. 2009. "Evangelical International Relations in the Postcolonial World: The Lausanne Movement and the Challenge of Diversity, 1974–89," *Missiology* 37, no. 3, 2009.

Charmaz, Kathy. 2006. *Constructing Grounded Theory: A Practical Guide through Qualitative Analysis.* London: Sage.

Chiang, Samuel, 2014. Catalyst for Orality and CEO of the Seed Company. June 5 interview in Manhattan Beach, CA.

Christianity Today 2010. https://www.christianitytoday.com/ct/2010/august/17.11.html (accessed 15 November 2015)

Claydon, David. 2004. "A New Vision, a New Heart, a Renewed Call." *Lausanne Occasional Papers,* 2004.

Cole, Neil. 2010. *Organic Leadership: Leading Naturally Right Where You Are.* Grand Rapids, MI: Baker.

Common Call, The. 2010. Scotland Assembly Hall, Edinburgh. June 6, 2010. Edinburgh Listening Group Report.

Conger, J.A. and Kanungo, R.N. *Charismatic Leadership in Organizations.* Thousand Oaks, CA: Sage, 1998.

Coon, Bradley A. and Gina A. Bellofatto 2011. "Review of 2010 Boston: The Changing Contours of World Mission and Christianity." *MissioNexus.*

Cullmann, Oscar. 1987. *Unity through Diversity: Its Foundation and a Contribution to the Discussion concerning the Possibilities of its Actualization,* trans. M. Eugene Boring. Minneapolis, MN: Fortress Press.

Dahle, Lars, Margunn Serigstad Dahle and Knud Jørgensen. 2014. *The Lausanne Movement: A Range of Perspectives.* Oxford: Regnum.

Deuel, Dave. 2018. Catalyst for Disabilities. June 23 emailed questionnaire.

Dietrich, Stephanie. 2018. "God's Mission as a Call for Transforming Unity: Call for Transforming Unity." *International Review of Mission* 107 (2), 378-390. https://www.researchgate.net/publication/329457670" God's_Mission_as_a_Call_for_Transforming_Unity_Call_for_Transformi ng_Unity" (accessed Nov 08 2019),

Dinh, J. E., Lord, R. G., Gardner, W. L., Meuser, J. D., Liden, R. C., and Hu, J. 2014. "Leadership Theory and Research in the New Millennium: Current Theoretical Trends and Changing Perspectives." *Leadership Quarterly,* 25 (1), 2014, 36-62.

Doll, Bob. 2018. Former chair of the board. August 24 interview via VOIP.

Downton, J. V. 1973. *Rebel Leadership: Commitment and Charisma in a Revolutionary Process.* New York: Free Press.

Escobar, Samuel. 1991. "A Movement Divided: Three Approaches to World Evangelization Stand in Tension with One Another," *Transformation,* 8.

Esler, Theodore. 2012. 'Movements and Missionary Agencies: A Case Study of Church Planting Missionary Teams.' Fuller Seminary Dissertation, March 2012.

Essamuah, Casely B. and David K. Ngaruiya, eds. 2013. "Communities of Faith in Africa and the African Diaspora. In Honor of Dr. Tite Tiénou with Additional Essays on World Christianity." Eugene, OR: Wipf & Stock.

Evans, Gary Llewellyn. 2013. "Culture Research and Corporate Boards." *American International Journal of Contemporary Research,* 3:5.

Fetterman, David M. 1989. *Ethnography: Step by Step.* Newbury Park, CA: Sage Publications.

Fiedler, F. E. 1964. "A Contingency Model of Leadership Effectiveness." In L. Berkowitz (ed.), *Advances in Experimental Social Psychology,* vol. 1. New York: Academic Press, 149-190.

Ford, Leighton, 2018. Former executive chair. 17 December 2018 interview via Skype.

Forsyth, T. and C. Johnson, 2014. "Elinor Ostrom's Legacy: Governing the Commons and the Rational Choice Controversy." Development and Change: Institute of Social Studies, The Hague, August 24, 2014.

Franke, G.R. and R.G. Richey, R.G. 2010. "Improving Generalizations from Multi-Country Comparisons in International Business Research." *Journal of International Business Studies,* Vol. 41, 1275–1293.

Franklin, Kirk. 2016. 'A Paradigm for Global Mission Leadership: The Journey of the Wycliffe Global Alliance.' Ph.D. University of Pretoria, 2016.

Franklin, Kirk, Dave Crough, and Deborah Crough. 2017. *Towards Global Missional Leadership: A Journey through Leadership Paradigm Shift in the Mission of God.* Oxford: Regnum.

Franklin, Kirk and Niemandt, N., 2016, "Polycentrism in the *Missio Dei,*" HTS Teologiese Studies/Theological Studies 72 (2), 2016.

.Frans Johansson. 2004. *The Medici Effect: Breakthrough Insights at the Intersection of Ideas, Concepts, and Cultures.* Boston, MA: Harvard Business School Press.

Friedman, Thomas. 2005. *The World is Flat: A Brief History of the Twenty-First Century.* New York: Farrar, Straus and Giroux.

Fung, Patrick. Board Member. 2018. August 19 interview in Singapore (OMF Center)

Fung, Patrick. 2016. "Cooperation in a Polycentric World." A Presentation at WEA, MC Global Consultation, Panama, 2.

García-Schmidt, Nydia. 2017. "Community Empowerment," in Franklin, Kirk J., Dave Crough, and Deborah Crough. *Towards Global Missional Leadership: A Journey Through Leadership Paradigm Shift in the Mission of God.* Oxford: Regnum.

Garland, David. 2003. *1 Corinthians*. Baker Exegetical Commentary on the New Testament. Grand Rapids, MI: Baker Academic.

Gibbs, Graham. 2007. *Analyzing Qualitative Data*. Los Angeles, CA: Sage Publications.

Gidoomal, Ram. 2015. Former chair of the board. February 5 interview via skype.

Glaser, Barney and Anselm Strauss. 1967. *The Discovery of Grounded Theory: Strategies for Qualitative Research*. Piscataway, NY: Aldine Transaction.

Global Trends 2030: Citizens in an Interconnected and Polycentric World report of the European Strategy and Policy Analysis System. Paris: Institute for Security Studies European Union.

Green, Stanley. 2011. "A Report on Cape Town 2010." *International Bulletin of Mission Research,* 35:2, April 2011, 7.

Greenman, Jeffrey, and Joshua Little. 2010. *Social Responsibility and Evangelism in the Lausanne Movement: A Historical and Theological Analysis*. Joshua Little, cpo, 1604, 2010. (https://www.academia.edu/4832944/Social_Responsibility_and_Evangelism_in_the_Lausanne_Movement_-_A_Historical_and_Theological_Analysis, p. 14 (accessed 15 November, 2015).

Greenleaf, R.K. 1970. *The Servant as Leader*. Westfield, IN: Center for Servant Leadership, 15 ff.

Grenz, Stanley J. 2001. *The Social God and the Relational Self: A Trinitarian Theory of the Imago Dei*. Louisville, KY: Westminster John Knox Press, 332.

Guest, G. 2013. "Describing Mixed Methods Research: An Alternative to Typologies." *Journal of Mixed Methods Research*, 7.

Hanciles, Jehu J. 2008. *Beyond Christendom: Globalization, African Migration, and the Transformation of the West*. Maryknoll, NY: Orbis Books.

Handley, Joseph. 2018. "Leading Mission Movements." *Evangelical Missions Quarterly (EMQ),* 20-27.

_____. 2021. "Polycentric Leadership: A Leadership Model for a Polarized World," *Outcomes Magazine*: Christian Leadership Alliance, Spring 2021 – https://outcomesmagazine.com/polycentric-leadership/ (accessed on 6 March 2021).

Hansen, Morton and Scott Tapp. 2010. "Who should be Your Chief Collaboration Officer?" *Harvard Business Review,* October 11, 2010. https://hbr.org/2010/10/who-should-be-your-chief-colla (accessed 23 February 2020).

Heifetz, Ronald, and Marty Linsky. 2002. *Leadership on the Line: Staying Alive through the Dangers of Leading*. Boston, MA: Harvard Business Press.

Heifitz, Robert. M. Linskey and A. Grashow. 2009. *The Practice of Adaptive Leadership*. Boston, MA: Harvard Business Press.

Hermann, Adrian and Ciprian Burlacioiu. 2016. "Current Debates About the Approach of the "Munich School" and Further Perspectives on the Interdisciplinary Study of the History of World Christianity." *Journal of World Christianity* 6 (1), 2016.

Hermann, Adrian. 2014. "Transnational Networks of Philippine Intellectuals." In Koschorke, Klaus and Hermann, Adrian. *Polycentric Structures in the History of World Christianity*. Berlin: Harrassowitz Verlag.

Hersey, P., and Blanchard, K. H. 1969a. "Life-Cycle Theory of Leadership." *Training and Development Journal*, 23, 26–34.

_____. 1969. "Management of Organizational Behavior utilizing Human Resources." *Academy of Management Journal*, 12 (4), 526.

Hesselbein, Frances. 2002. *Hesselbein on Leadership*. San Francisco, CA: Jossey-Bass.

Hesselgrave, David F., Donald McGavran, and Jeff Reed. 1978. *Planting Churches Cross-Culturally: North America and Beyond*. 2nd ed. Grand Rapids, MI: Baker Academic.

Hirsch, Alan. 2007. *The Forgotten Ways: Reactivating the Missional Church*. Ada, MI: Brazos Press.

Hjalmarson, Len. 2013. "The Trinitarian Nature of Leadership." *Crucible Theology and Ministry,* 5:2 November 2013.

Hofstede, G. 1980. *Culture's Consequences: International Differences in Work-Related Values*. Beverly Hills, CA: Sage.

Hofstede, G. 2001. *Culture's Consequences: Comparing Values, Behaviors, Institutions, and Organizations Across Nations*. Thousand Oaks, CA: Sage.

Hofstede, G. 2010. "The GLOBE Debate: Back to Relevance." *Journal of International Business Studies*, 41, 8, 1339-1346.

Hofstede, G. 2006. "What Did GLOBE really Measure? Researchers' Minds versus Respondents' Minds." *Journal of International Business Studies*, 37, 6, 882–896.

Hofstede, G., and G.J. Hofstede, G. J. 2005. *Cultures and Organizations: Software of the Mind.* 2nd ed., New York: McGraw-Hill.

Hollenweger, Walter. 1006. 'From Azusa to the Toronto Phenomenon: Historical Roots of the Pentecostal Movement', in Jürgen Moltmann and Karl-Josef Kuschel (eds.), *Pentecostal Movements as Ecumenical Challenge*. London: SCM, 1996.

Holstein, James A., and Jaber F. Gubrium. 1995. *The Active Interview*. Thousand Oaks, CA: Sage Publications.

Homola, Milan.2008. "Unitarian Relational Leadership: The Myth!" http://consumingjesus.org/wp- content/milan_homola_-_trintarian_leadership.pdf. (accessed 23 February, 2020).

House, Robert and Jagdeep Chhokar and Felix Broadbeck. 2007. *Culture and Leadership Across the World: The GLOBE Book of In-Depth Studies of 25 Societies.* London: Psychology Press.

House, Robert and Paul Hanges, Mansour Javidian, Peter Dorfmann and Peter Gupta. 2004. *Culture, Leadership, and Organizations: The GLOBE Study of 62 Societies.* Thousand Oaks, CA: Sage.

House, Robert J. Peter W. Dorfman, Mansour Javidian, Paul J. Hanges, and Mary F. Sully de Luque. 2014. *Strategic Leadership Across Cultures: The GLOBE Study of CEO Leadership Behavior and Effectiveness in 24 Countries.* Thousand Oaks, CA: Sage.

House, Robert. A. 1976. 'Theory of Charismatic Leadership.' Working Paper Series 76-06. University of Toronto, October 1976.

Hunt, Robert. 2011. "The History of the Lausanne Movement, 1974-2011." *International Bulletin of Mission Research,* 35:2, April 2011.

Hustedde, R., 2007, "What's Culture got to do with it? Strategies for Strengthening Entrepreneurial Culture", in N. Walzer, *Entrepreneurship and Local Economic Development.* Plymouth: Lexington Books, 39-58.

Iaocca, Lee. 1998. *Talking Straight.* London: Bantam.

Javidan, M. Teagarden, M., Bowen, D. 2010. "Making it Overseas." *Harvard Business Review.* April, 109-115.

Jenkins, Philip. 2016. "Book Review: The Unexpected Christian Century: The Reversal and Transformation of Global Christianity, 1900–2000". *International Bulletin of Mission Research,* 40 (1), 84-86.

Johansson, Frans. 2004. *The Medici Effect: Breakthrough Insights at the Intersection of Ideas, Concepts, and Cultures.* Boston, MA: Harvard Business School Press.

Jones, Candace, Hesterly and Borgatti. 1997. "A general theory of network governance: Exchange conditions and social mechanisms." *Academy of Management Review*, vol. 22, 1997.

Jørgensen, Knud. 2014. "Edinburgh, Tokyo and Cape Town: Comparing and Contrasting on the way to 2010." In *The Lausanne Movement: A Range of Perspectives*. Lars and Margunn Dahle (eds.) along with Knud Jørgensen. Oxford: Regnum.

Kennedy, John W. 2010. "The Most Diverse Gathering Ever." *Christianity Today*, September 2010. http://www.christianitytoday.com/ct/2010/september/34.66.html (accessed 16 November 2015).

Kim, Kirsteen. 2017. Book Review, *Themelios,* 42 (2), 2017. http://themelios.thegospelcoalition.org/review/polycentric-missiology-twenty-first-century-mission (accessed 23 February 2020).

Kinnamon, Michael. 1997. *The Ecumenical Movement: An Anthology of Key Texts and Voices.* Grand Rapids, MI: Eerdmans.

Kogler Hill, Susan. 2015. 'Team Leadership Model.' In Northouse, Peter *Leadership: Theory and Practice.* Thousand Oaks, CA: Sage, 287-318.

Koschorke, Klaus and Adrian Hermann. 2014. *Polycentric Structures in the History of World Christianity.* Berlin: Harrassowitz Verlag.

Koschorke, Klaus. "New Maps of the History of World Christianity: Current Challenges and Future Perspectives." *Theology Today* 7 (2), 2014.

Kostansky, Paul.2015. September 23 interview in Orlando, FL.

Kouzes, James M., and Barry Z. Posner. 1995. *The Leadership Challenge: How to Keep Getting Extraordinary Things Done in Organizations*. San Francisco, CA: Jossey-Bass.

Kuhn, T., 2012, *The Structure of Scientific Revolutions*, 50th Anniversary Edition. Chicago, IL: University of Chicago Press.

Küng, H., 1988, *Theology for the Third Millennium*. New York: Anchor Books.

Kvale, Steinar. 2007. *Doing Interviews*. London: Sage Publications.

Ladner, Sam. 2014. *Practical Ethnography*. Oxford: Routledge.

Lalsingkima Pachuau. 2009. "Missionaries Sent and Received, Asia, 1910-2010." in Johnson, Todd and Kenneth Ross *Atlas of Global Christianity*. Edinburgh: Edinburgh University Press.

Laniak, Timothy. 2006. *Shepherds after My Own Heart: Pastoral Traditions and Leadership in the Bible*. Downers Grove, IL: IVP Press.

Larson, C. E., and LaFasto, F. M. J. 1989. *Teamwork: What must go Right/What can go Wrong*. Newbury Park, CA: Sage.

Latourette, Kenneth Scott. 1938. *A History of the Expansion of Christianity: The Great Century, A.D. 1800-A.D. 1914, Europe and the United States of America*. New York: Harper and Brothers.

_____. 1954. "Ecumenical Bearings of the Missionary Movement and the International Missionary Council" in Ruth Rouse and Stephen C. Neill, eds., *A History of the Ecumenical Movement,* Vol. 1. Geneva: World Council of Churches.

Lausanne Movement Mission and Vision Statements: https://www.lausanne.org/about-the-movement (accessed 12 March 2020).

Lausanne Movement Website: http://www.lausanne.org/about-the-movement (accessed 23 February 2020).

Lausanne Occasional Paper 21.1982. 'Evangelism and Social Responsibility: An Evangelical Commitment.' A Joint Publication of the Lausanne Committee for World Evangelization and the World Evangelical Fellowship. Grand Rapids, MI, 1982. https://www.lausanne.org/content/lop/lop-21. (Accessed 15 November, 2015).

Lausanne Website, https://www.lausanne.org/content/whole-gospel-whole-church-whole-world (accessed 9 September 2019).

Lederleitner, Mary. 2016. Plenary Address: 'Polycentric Missiology.' The 14th annual Global Consultation in Panama - WEA Mission Commission: The 14th Global Consultation of the World Evangelical Alliance Mission Commission. October 3-7, 2016. https://www.worldea.org/news/4723/wea-mission-commission-highlights-polycentric-mission-during-panama-global-consultation.

Leedy, Paul D., and Jeanne Ellis Ormrod. 2013. *Practical Research: Planning and Design*. Upper Saddle River, NJ: Pearson Education.

Lehmann, Hartmut. 2014. "Polyzentrische Strukturen in der Geschichte des Weltchristentums als Forschungsprogramm. Ein Kommentar." Berlin: Harrassowitz Verlag.

Levi, D. 2011. *Group Dynamics for Teams*. Thousand Oaks, CA: Sage.

Liden, R. C., Wayne, S. J., Zhao, H., and Henderson, D. 2008. "Servant Leadership: Development of a Multidimensional Measure and Multi-Level Assessment." *Leadership Quarterly*, 19, 161-177.

Lienemann, Wolfgang. 2014. "Die Christenheit in der Weltgesellschaft. Kommentar und Fragen zu einem Forschungsprogramm. Polycentric Structures in the History of World Christianity. Berlin: Harrassowitz Verlag.

Lindsay, D. Michael. 2014. 'Platinum Study.' https://www.gordon.edu/platinumstudy (emailed July 24, 2014)

Lingenfelter, Sherwood. 2008. *Leading Cross-Culturally: Covenant Relationships for Effective Christian Leadership*. Grand Rapids, MI: Baker, 2008.

Logan, Dave, John King, and Halee Fischer-Wright. 2008. *Tribal Leadership*. New York: Harper Collins.

Lord, R.G. and Maher, K.J. 1990. "Alternative Information Processing Models and their Implication for Theory, Research, and Practice." *Academy of Management Review,* 15 (1): 9-28.

_____. 1991. *Leadership and Information Processing: Linking Perceptions and Performance*. Boston, MA: Unwin Hyman.

Maliuta, Ruslan. 2018. Children at Risk Network. 7 March 2018 interview via Skype

Manila Manifesto. 1989. https://www.lausanne.org/content/manifesto/the-manila-manifesto (accessed 17 February, 2020)

Mankin, D., Cohen, S. G., and Bikson, T. K. 1996. *Teams and Technology*. Boston, MA: Harvard Business School Press.

Martin, Rob. 2018. Former US Director and Senior Associate for Global Philanthropy. August 24 interview via Skype.

Maxwell, David. 2017. "Historical Perspectives on Christianity Worldwide: Connections, Comparisons and Consciousness." *Theology and Mission in World Christianity*, v. 7, eds. Cabrita, Maxwell, and Wild-Wood. Leiden: Brill.

Maxwell, Joseph Alex. 1996. *Qualitative Research Design: An Interactive Approach*. Thousand Oaks, CA: Sage Publications.

Mayer, John, Salovey, Peter, and Caruso, David. 2004. "Emotional Intelligence: Theory, Findings and Implications." *Psychological Inquiry* 2004, 15:3.

McChrystal, Stanley, David Silverman, Tantum Collins, Chris Fusell. 2015. *Team of Teams: New Rules of Engagement for a Complex World.* New York: Penguin Random House.

McConnell, C. Douglas. 2018. *Cultural Insights for Christian Leaders*. Grand Rapids, MI: Baker.

_____. 2019 Response on 3 December.

McDonald, Patrick. 2018. Former Catalyst for Children at Risk. September 25 interview in Oxford, England.

McGrath, Alister. 2001. *Christian Theology: An Introduction*, 3rd ed. Oxford: Blackwell.

McKinney, Carol Virginia. 2000. *Globetrotting in Sandals: A Field Guide to Cultural Research*. Dallas, TX: SIL.

McManus, Erwin. 2001. *An Unstoppable Force: Daring to become the Church God had in Mind*. Colorado Springs, CO: David C. Cook.

McNeal, Reggie. 2009. *The Present Future: Six Tough Questions for the Church*. San Francisco, CA: Jossey-Bass, 2009.

McNeil, Reggie. *Practicing Greatness: 7 Disciplines of Extraordinary Spiritual Leaders*. San Francisco, CA: Jossey-Bass, 2006.

Moffett, Samuel. 2005. *The History of Christianity in Asia*. Maryknoll, NY: Orbis.

Moltmann, Jürgen. 2000. *Trinity in the Kingdom of God*. London: SCM.

Morse, Suzanne. 1998. "Five Building Blocks for Successful Leadership," in *The Community of the Future*, ed. Frances Hesselbein et al. San Francisco, CA: Jossey-Bass.

Neill, Stephen C. 2009. *History of the Ecumenical Movement*, 3v. (Vol. 1-2: eds. Ruth Rouse and Stephen Neill.) Eugene, OR: Wipf & Stock.

Newbigin, Lesslie. 1995. *The Open Secret: An Introduction to the Theology of Mission*, rev. ed. Grand Rapids, MI: Eerdmans.

Newman, Las. 2019. Global Associate Director for Regions. December 20 emailed response with follow up call via Skype.

Ng, Peter Tze Ming. 2014. "The Making of Modern China: Reflections on the Role of Chinese YMCA Christians who returned from Japan and the US in the early 20th Century." In Koschorke, Klaus and Hermann, Adrian. *Polycentric Structures in the History of World Christianity*. Berlin: Harrassowitz Verlag.

Northouse, Peter. 2013. *Leadership: Theory and Practice*. Thousand Oaks, CA: Sage.

Oh, Michael. 2015. CEO December 9 interview in King of Prussia, PA.

Oladipo, Caleb O. 2013. "How Indigenous Traders Brought Christianity to Northern Nigeria." In Essamuah, Casely B. and David K. Ngaruiya, eds., *Communities of Faith in Africa and the African Diaspora: In Honor of Dr. Tite Tiénou with Additional Essays on World Christianity*. Eugene, OR: Wipf & Stock.

Olesberg, Lindsay. 2018. Catalyst for Scripture Engagement and Scripture Engagement Director for InterVarsity. July 20 interview via Skype.

Olesen, Virginia. 2007. "Feminist Qualitative Research and Grounded Theory: Complexities, Criticisms, and Opportunities." In A. Bryant, and K. Charmaz eds. *The SAGE Handbook of Grounded Theory*. London: Sage, 417-436.
doi: http://dx.doi.org/10.4135/9781848607941.n19.

Ostrom, Elinor. 1990. *Governing the Commons: The Evolution of Institutions for Collective Action.* Cambridge: Cambridge University Press.

_____. June 2010. "Beyond Markets and States: Polycentric Governance of Complex Economic Systems." *American Economic Review*, 100 (3): 641-72.

Padilla, Rene. 1976. *The New Face of Evangelicalism.* Downers Grove, IL: InterVarsity.

_____. 2011. "The Future of the Lausanne Movement." *International Bulletin of Mission Research,* 35:2, April 2011.

Parrott, Roger. 2018/ former Lausanne board member and president of Bellhaven University. June 29 interview via Skype.

Peterson, Jonathan. 2016. Interview with Scott Sunquist about his book *The Unexpected Christian Century*. April 2016. https://www.biblegateway.com/blog/2016/04/the-unexpected-christian-century-an-interview-with-scott-sunquist/ (accessed 15 November 2017).

Pier, Mac. 2019. Catalyst for Cities. July 19 interview via phone.

Pierson, Paul. 2009. *The Dynamics of Christian Mission.* Pasadena, CA: William Carey University Press. 2009, 135-149.

Pillette, Bard. 1996. "Paul and His Fellow Workers." *Emmaus*, 6, 1, 119-128.

Plueddemann, James. 2012. *Leading Across Cultures.* Downers Grove, IL: IVP Academic.

Polanyi, Michael. 2013. *The Logic of Liberty.* London: International Library of Sociology.

Rao, Narayana. 2012. "What is the Difference between Proposition and Hypothesis." Online Resource, accessed February 17, 2020.

Robert, Dana. 2016. "One Christ – Many Witnesses: Visions of Mission and Unity, Edinburgh and Beyond." *Transformation,* 33,4, 2016, October, 270-281.

Roser, Max. 2020. "Democracy". Published online at OurWorldInData.org. (accessed 12, March, 2020).

Ross, Kenneth R. 2009. 'From Edinburgh 1910 to Edinburgh 2010.' In Mogens Mogensen (ed.), *Edinburgh 1910 – 100 år efter.* København: Dansk Missionsråd.

Ross, Kenneth, and David Kerr. 2009. "The Commissions after a Century." In *Edinburgh 2010: Mission Then and Now.* Oxford: Regnum Books.

Roxburgh, Alan, J. and Fred Romanuk. 2006. *The Missional Leader, Equipping Your Church to Reach a Changing World.* San Francisco, CA: Jossey-Bass.

Saee, John. 2005. Effective Leadership for the Global Economy in the 21st Century. *Journal of Business Economics and Management*, 6:1, 3-11.

Sakai, Y.Y., Sugano T., Maeda T. 2007. *Introduction of Toyota Production System to promote innovative manufacturing, Fujitsu Science Technology Japan*, no. 43, 14–22, January 2007, http://www.fujitsu.com.

Salas, E., G. F. Goodwin, and C. S. Burke eds. 2009. *Team Effectiveness in Complex Organizations: Cross–disciplinary Perspectives and Approaches.* New York: Taylor & Francis, 83-111.

Samson-Song, Grace. 2018. Board member. July 1 emailed questionnaire.

Sanneh, Lamin. 2005. *The Changing Face of Christianity: Africa, the West, and the World.* Oxford: Oxford University Press.

Schein, Edgar H. 1985. *Organizational Culture and Leadership.* San Francisco, CA: Jossey-Bass.

Schneider, Mark, John Scholz, Mark Lubell, Denisa Mindruta, and Matthew Edwardsen. 2003. "Building Consensual Institutions: Networks and the National Estuary Program." *American Journal of Political Science*, 47, 1.

Scholte, Jan Aart. 2004. "Globalization and Governance: From Statism to Polycentrism." *Globalization: A Critical Introduction.* London: Red Globe Press.

Schreiter, Robert. 2011. "From the Lausanne Movement to Cape Town Commitment." *International Bulletin of Mission Research,* 35:2.

Shamir, B., and G. Eilam. 2005. 'Authentic Leadership Measurement and Development: Challenges and Suggestions.' In Gardner, W.L., B.J. Avolio and F.O. Walumbwa. *Leadership Theory and Practice: Origins, Effects and Development.* Oxford: Elsevier Science, 227-251.

_____. 2005. "What's your story? A life-stories approach to authentic leadership development." *Leadership Quarterly*, 16, 395–417.

Shamir, Boaz, Robert House and Michael Arthur. 1993. "The Motivational Effects of Charismatic Leadership: A Self-Concept Based Theory." *Organizational Science.* 4:4.

Shaw, R. Daniel and Jonathan Grimes. 2012. 'Methods of Interpreting Culture course at Fuller Seminary.' Fall, 2012.

Shaw, R. Daniel. 2012. 'Syllabus for Methods of Observing and Interpreting Culture.' Fall, 2012, 28.

Shenk, Wilbert. 2005. "2004 Forum for World Evangelization: A Report," *International Bulletin of Missionary Research* 29,1, 31.

Sivers, D. 2010. *How to start a Movement.* TED Talk, YouTube. https://www.ted.com/talks/derek_sivers_how_to_start_a_movement accessed September 2015.

Skjøtt, Bodil. 2018. Catalyst for Jewish Evangelism. June 29 interview via Skype.

Smith, Brad. 2010. Table Group Facilitator – Cape Town 2010. 11 December 2014 interview via Skype.

Snodgrass, Klyne. 1996. *Ephesians: The NIV Application Commentary.* Grand Rapids, MI: Zondervan.

Spears, L. C. 2002. "Tracing the past, present, and future of servant-leadership." In L. C. Spears and M. Lawrence eds., *Focus on Leadership: Servant-Leadership for the 21st Century.* New York: John Wiley & Sons.

Spradley, James P. 1979. *The Ethnographic Interview.* New York: Holt, Rinehart and Winston, 1-16.

Spradlin, Byron. 2014. Catalyst for the Arts. December 15 interview via
   Skype.
Stake, Robert. 1995. *The Art of Case Study Research*. Thousand Oaks, CA:
   Sage.
Steuernagel, Valdir R. 1975. "Social Concern and Evangelization: The
   Journey of the Lausanne Movement." *International Bulletin of Missionary
   Research* 15, no. 2.
Stevens, R. Paul. 1999. *The Other Six Days*. Grand Rapids, MI: Eerdmans.
Stott, John. 1975. *Lausanne Covenant, 1974 Lausanne Covenant: Complete
   Text with Study Guide*. Peabody, MA: Hendrickson (published 2012).
_____. 1995. "Twenty Years after Lausanne: Some Personal Reflections."
   International Bulletin of Missionary Research 19, no. 2.
_____. 1995. "Significance of Lausanne," *International Review of Mission*
   64, no. 255.
Stracke, E., and Kumar, V. 2010. "Feedback and Self-Regulated Learning:
   Insights from Supervisors' and PhD Examiners' Reports." *Reflective
   Practice*, 11 (1), 19–32.
Sunquist, Scott. 2017. Book Review, *International Bulletin of Mission
   Research* 41 (4) 2017.
Taylor, Frederick Winslow. 2010. *The Principles of Scientific Management*.
   Scotts Valley, CA: CreateSpace Independent Publishing Platform.
Tennent, Timothy. 2014. *The Lausanne Movement: A Range of Perspectives*.
   In Lars and Margunn Serigstad Dahl eds. along with Knud Jørgensen.
   Oxford: Regnum.
Tenney, Merrill, 1984. *The Expositors Bible Commentary: John and Acts*.
   Grand Rapids, MI: Zondervan, (accessed via Accordance Bible Software,
   15 December 2019).
Thornton, J.K. 1998. *Africa and Africans in the Making of the Atlantic
   World, 1400–1800*. Cambridge: Cambridge University Press.
TIME Magazine and Newsweek:
   https://www.lausanne.org/content/lga/2014-07/lausanne-74 (accessed 17
   February, 2020).
Tira, Sadiri Joy. 2014. Global Diaspora Network. December 6.
_____. 2019. Interview via Skype – email on July 18.
Tunehag, Mats. 2014. Catalyst for Business as Mission. December 4
   interview via Skype.
Tung, R.L. and Verbeke, A. 2010. "Beyond Hofstede and GLOBE:
   Improving the Quality of Cross-Cultural Research." *Journal of
   International Business Studies*, vol. 41, 1259–1274.
Uhl-Bien, Mary, Russ Marion and Bill McKelvey. 2007. "Complexity
   Leadership Theory: Shifting Leadership from the Industrial Age to the
   Knowledge Era." *Leadership Quarterly*, 18:4, (August 2007), 298-318.
Van Engen, Charles. 1999 *Footprints of God: A Narrative Theology of
   Mission*. Monrovia, CA: MARC.
Vijayam, Joseph. 2018. Senior Associate for Technology and CEO of Olive
   Technology. August 2 interview via Zoom.

Volf, Miroslav. 1998. *After Our Likeness: The Church as the Image of the Trinity*. Grand Rapids, MI: Eerdmans.

Walker, Simon P. 2011. *The Undefended Leader Trilogy*. Oxford: Human Ecology Partners.

Walls, Andrew. 1996. *The Missionary Movement in Christian History: Studies in the Transmission of Faith*. Maryknoll, NY: Orbis Books.

_____. 2002. "Missiology," in *Dictionary of the Ecumenical Movement*. Geneva: WCC, 2002.

_____. 2016. "Sierra Leone, Afro-American Reimmigration and the Beginnings of Protestantism in West Africa", quoted in Koschorke, "Transcontinental Links, Enlarged Maps, and Polycentric Structures in the History of World Christianity." *Journal of World Christianity*, 6/1: 45-56.

Weber, Klaus and Brayden King. 2013. 'Social Movement Theory and Organization Studies.' In *Oxford Handbook of Sociology, Social Theory and Organization Studies*, Paul Adler, Paul du Gay, Glenn Morgan, Mike Reed (eds.), 9-10.

Welch, Jack. 2005. *Jack: Straight from the Gut*. London: Headline.

Whitacre, Rodney, John. 2010. The IVP New Testament Commentary Series (4) 2010. https://www.biblegateway.com/resources/commentaries/IVP-NT/John/Jesus-Concludes-Time-Alone.

Wilton, Gregory D. 2012. 'A Cluster Analysis of the Terms Evangelism and Mission in the 1974 Lausanne Covenant, the 1989 Manila Manifesto, and the 2010 Cape Town Commitment' Ph.D. dissertation, New Orleans Baptist Theological Seminary.

Winter, Ralph. 1997. "Four Men, Three Eras." *Mission Frontiers,* Sept 1997. http://www.missionfrontiers.org/issue/article/four-men-three-eras (accessed 14 November 2015).

Wong, Menchit. 2018. Personal Interview via skype, January 2018

_____. 2018. February 5 interview in Manila.

Woods, Paul. 2015. "Perichoresis and Koinonia: Implications of our Fellowship with God for the Changing Missions Endeavor." *Mission Round Table,* 10,1, January 2015.

Woodward, JR. 2013. *Creating a Missional Culture: Equipping the Church for the Sake of the World.* Downers Grove, IL: InterVarsity Press.

World Evangelical Alliance, Mission Commission Global Consultation: https://www.worldea.org/news/4723/wea-mission-commission-highlights-polycentric-mission-during-panama-global-consultation. (Accessed on October 21, 2019).

Wright, Christopher. 2006. *The Mission of God: Unlocking the Bible's Grand Narrative.* Downers Grove, IL: IVP Press.

_____. 2011. *The Cape Town Commitment: A Confession of Faith and a Call to Action.* Peabody, MA: Hendrickson.

_____. 2016. Former Theology Working Group. January19 interview via Skype.

Yeh, Allen. 2010. "Tokyo 2010 and Edinburgh 2010: A Comparison of Two Centenary Congresses." *International Journal of Frontier Missions,* 27:3, Fall, 2010.

_____. 2015. Interview at Biola University on February 4.

_____. 2016. *Polycentric Missiology: 21st Century Mission from Everyone to Everywhere.* Downers Grove, IL: IVP Academic.

_____. 2019. Note received on 21 October 2019.

Zaccaro, S.J., B. Heinen, and M. Shuffler. 2009. 'Team and Team Leadership and Team Effectiveness.' In E. Salas, G.F. Goodwin, and C.S. Burke eds. *Team Effectiveness in Complex Organizations: Cross-Disciplinary Perspectives and Approaches.* New York: Taylor & Francis, 83-111.

Zald, M.N., and R Ash. 1966. "Social Movement Organizations: Growth, Decay and Change." *Social Forces,* 44 (3): 327-341

Zaretsky, Tuvya. 2014. December 2 interview via Skype.

Zscheile, Dwight. 2007. "The Trinity, Leadership and Power." *Journal of Religious Leadership,* 6, 2, Fall, 2007.